THE **COMPLETE IDIOT'S GUIDE** TO

Boosting Employee Performance

by Marc Dorio and Susan Shelly

D1318679

ALPHA

A member of Penguin Group (USA) Inc.

ALPHA BOOKS

Published by the Penguin Group

Penguin Group (USA) Inc., 375 Hudson Street, New York, New York 10014, USA

Penguin Group (Canada), 90 Eglinton Avenue East, Suite 700, Toronto, Ontario M4P 2Y3, Canada (a division of Pearson Penguin Canada Inc.)

Penguin Books Ltd., 80 Strand, London WC2R 0RL, England

Penguin Ireland, 25 St. Stephen's Green, Dublin 2, Ireland (a division of Penguin Books Ltd.)

Penguin Group (Australia), 250 Camberwell Road, Camberwell, Victoria 3124, Australia (a division of Pearson Australia Group Pty. Ltd.)

Penguin Books India Pvt. Ltd., 11 Community Centre, Panchsheel Park, New Delhi—110 017, India

Penguin Group (NZ), 67 Apollo Drive, Rosedale, North Shore, Auckland 1311, New Zealand (a division of Pearson New Zealand Ltd.)

Penguin Books (South Africa) (Pty.) Ltd., 24 Sturdee Avenue, Rosebank, Johannesburg 2196, South Africa

Penguin Books Ltd., Registered Offices: 80 Strand, London WC2R 0RL, England

Copyright © 2011 by Marc Dorio and Susan Shelly

International Standard Book Number: 978-1-61564-025-6
Library of Congress Catalog Card Number: 2010908789

13   12   11   8   7   6   5   4   3   2

Interpretation of the printing code: The rightmost number of the first series of numbers is the year of the book's printing; the rightmost number of the second series of numbers is the number of the book's printing. For example, a printing code of 11-1 shows that the first printing occurred in 2011.

Printed in the United States of America

Note: This publication contains the opinions and ideas of its authors. It is intended to provide helpful and informative material on the subject matter covered. It is sold with the understanding that the authors and publisher are not engaged in rendering professional services in the book. If the reader requires personal assistance or advice, a competent professional should be consulted.

The authors and publisher specifically disclaim any responsibility for any liability, loss, or risk, personal or otherwise, which is incurred as a consequence, directly or indirectly, of the use and application of any of the contents of this book.

Most Alpha books are available at special quantity discounts for bulk purchases for sales promotions, premiums, fund-raising, or educational use. Special books, or book excerpts, can also be created to fit specific needs.

For details, write: Special Markets, Alpha Books, 375 Hudson Street, New York, NY 10014.

Publisher: *Marie Butler-Knight*
Associate Publisher: *Mike Sanders*
Senior Managing Editor: *Billy Fields*
Senior Acquisitions Editor: *Paul Dinas*
Development Editor: *Lynn Northrup*
Senior Production Editor: *Janette Lynn*

Copy Editor: *Krista Hansing Editorial Services, Inc.*
Cover Designer: *Kurt Owens*
Book Designers: *William Thomas, Rebecca Batchelor*
Indexer: *Brad Herriman*
Layout: *Ayanna Lacey*
Proofreader: *Laura Caddell*

Contents

Foreword

Perhaps the most important management lesson we've learned over the years at Marotta Controls is that we're still learning.

What we do know is that, whether your organization has 2 or 2,000 employees, there are jobs to get done, bosses to please, rules to follow, and a culture that must be learned and adapted to. How well we perform in our jobs influences the success of those around us and impacts the mission and goals of the organization.

We have learned the importance of establishing performance standards and expectations for our employees, and of training, coaching, and reviewing performance. We realize that our employees are our most expensive and valuable assets, and that by taking time to train, establish thoughtful communication, and reinforce the company's culture, we can reduce turnover, build employee loyalty, improve morale, and ultimately satisfy our customers more quickly than the competition.

Much of our employee success can be attributed to the fact that, every day, our managers apply the information and techniques in this book. The book demonstrates that doing our jobs well is less about the actual work than it is about knowing what is expected and satisfying that need. Problems arise when the exact output is not described and we do what we *think* is expected.

In *The Complete Idiot's Guide to Boosting Employee Performance*, management consultant and author Marc Dorio shares his years of business experience, along with his keen insights into coaching and managing employees, to help you make sure your employees perform at the top of their game, not only meeting, but exceeding your standards and expectations. Using the tools he introduces and equips you to use, you will be able to shape your business culture and, ultimately, boost the performance of your entire organization.

We have found the advice of this book to be practical, hands-on, and extremely useful. Managers must set the tone for workplace improvements by coaching employees to achieve higher goals. Every employee must be challenged—and rewarded when improvements are achieved and goals are met or exceeded. Using Dorio's advice and acting on his insights, your working managers will be able to harness the benefits of cooperation and boost employee performance.

Thomas S. Marotta, Chairman and CEO
Patrick A. Marotta, President and COO
Marotta Controls, Inc., Montville, N.J.

Introduction

The Complete Idiot's Guide to Boosting Employee Performance is a guide for busy managers who want to improve their management skills and get the most from their employees by keeping them motivated and committed to the mission and goals of the organization.

Whether you manage 3, 30, or 300 employees, this book will help you understand what members of your team need from you, and how you can best meet those needs and keep them performing to their best abilities.

How This Book Is Organized

The book contains 23 chapters organized under 5 parts, with an appendix of helpful resources. It is intended to be used in the way that works best for you. You can start at the beginning and read it through, or pick out the parts that most apply to your situation and concentrate first on those.

Part 1, The Building Blocks, introduces you to common myths that some managers buy into and tells you why they don't hold up when you take time to examine them. You'll learn that employees really want to understand exactly what they're expected to do, how they're supposed to do it, and how their work fits into the bigger picture. This part also fills you in on the basics of performance management and walks you through the four steps of the performance management cycle. Finally, you'll learn how important it is to clearly define exactly what you expect from your employees.

Part 2, Monitor and Assess Performance, tells you why it's so important to keep in touch with your employees and to give them regular feedback on how they're doing. Feedback is an excellent tool for keeping employees motivated, but it must be given properly to be effective. You'll also learn how to help average employees become good employees by boosting their job performance, and how to increase the performances of good employees to make them great employees. This part also provides pointers on recognizing and correcting common performance problems and on dealing with problem employees. Difficult behavior occurs for a variety of reasons, which means it's important to recognize it and work with employees to get their behaviors, and performances, back on track.

Part 3, Tools for Boosting Performance, shows you which tools might be available and how to best use them. These tools might include providing training and development to motivate employees and invest them in their jobs, using performance actions plans, or connecting employees with customers to link them to the bigger picture and increase their pride in their jobs. You'll also learn the importance of an employee's first 90 days of employment, and the steps you need to take to get new employees off to a strong start.

Part 4, Performance and Reward, shows you that performance reviews don't have to be the nightmare they are for many managers—or employees. Performance reviews are useful and necessary, and when they're prepared for and conducted properly, they can be nearly painless. Development plans are a great means of helping valued employees advance within the organization, so you'll learn when and how to use them and how to follow up. This part also deals with employee compensation, both monetary and nonmonetary, and how both types can be used to recognize and reward employees for performance. Part 4 wraps up with a discussion on the importance of being willing to delegate work and responsibility to your employees, and the benefits that can result from you doing so.

Part 5, Leadership Challenges, takes on the issues of shepherding employees through good times and tough times. A manager who has guided employees through the recession of the latter part of the first decade of the 2000s is likely to be surprised to read that managing in good times also includes challenges. Don't worry, though—when those good times return, you'll be prepared. Every manager has a particular style of leadership that seems more natural than other styles. In this part, though, you'll learn that it's important to recognize a variety of leadership styles and know when it's appropriate to use each one. You'll also read about the attributes of an effective leader and how to develop those tendencies in your managerial style. And you'll get a feel for the challenges of managing more than one generation of workers; some organizations have four generations working together. You'll learn how to encourage unity and productivity.

Because you'll be motivated to learn more after finishing this book, we've included a resource of additional reading and useful websites.

Extras

In addition to useful advice and information, you'll find three different types of sidebars sprinkled throughout the chapters:

PERFORMANCE GAP

These boxes warn you of common mistakes, misconceptions about employee performance, and other areas that could affect your efforts to boost your employees' performance.

PERFORMANCE BOOST

These boxes contain helpful tips and miscellaneous information on working more effectively with employees and motivating them to improve performance.

CASE IN POINT

These boxes include case histories and real stories, to illustrate a point or give you additional information.

Acknowledgements

I would like to thank my many clients within whose organizations I have been privileged to work. The knowledge I've acquired in working with the talented managers and employees in those companies forms the basis for what I've shared in this book.

Also, thanks to Edward B. Claflin, my literary agent, whose guidance and patience is always appreciated. I'd like to acknowledge the skilled and professional work of Susan Shelly, who collaborated on the writing of this work; and the editors at Alpha Books, who provided expertise and direction.

Most of all, my thanks to my wife, Patricia, whose love and support is beyond infinite.

Susan Shelly is a freelance writer, researcher, and editorial consultant. A former newspaper reporter and columnist, her other works have included corporate histories, guides to networking and business research, and *The Complete Idiot's Guide® to Personal Finance in Your 20s and 30s, Fourth Edition*.

Trademarks

All terms mentioned in this book that are known to be or are suspected of being trademarks or service marks have been appropriately capitalized. Alpha Books and Penguin Group (USA) Inc. cannot attest to the accuracy of this information. Use of a term in this book should not be regarded as affecting the validity of any trademark or service mark.

The Building Blocks

Most employees care about their work and want to perform their jobs well. To do that, though, they need to understand exactly what they're supposed to do, how to do it, and why they're doing it. That's where you come in. Part 1 teaches you about the importance of clearly communicating your expectations to your employees and making sure they understand them. You'll also learn what not to believe about your employees, and you'll check out the performance management cycle, an effective method of moving employees forward.

What to Know About Your Employees

In This Chapter

- Common myths about employees
- What employees want from you
- Using the tools you already have to motivate workers

The fact that you've picked up this book to learn more about your employees and how you can motivate them to be the best workers possible says a lot about you as a manager. It says that you're open to learning and aren't afraid of new ideas and strategies. It says that you care about your employees and want them to be the best workers they can be. And it says that, if you're willing to consider and implement the plans that you read about in this book, you'll succeed in boosting employee performance.

Many managers buy into common myths about employees, such as that all they want is a paycheck, or that they know full well what they're supposed to do but don't do it anyway. In this chapter, you'll learn why those myths don't hold up, what your employees need from you, and what you need to do to make sure employees have the tools they need to succeed.

Let's clarify something right from the beginning. While some managers feel they've got to be tough and hard in order to keep employees in line, there's nothing strange or wrong with wanting to empower your employees to do and be the best they can. There's nothing "soft" about coaching your employees, nothing sissy about mentoring or providing feedback. Business leaders for decades have recognized the need to be responsive to employees, to consider leadership style when working with different employees, and to earn the respect of their teams. I've worked with managers on factory floors, in executive offices, and in about every setting in between. Good management is good management, and your employees will respond to it and want to give you their best. Let's get started.

Don't Buy into These Employee Myths

As I've worked with managers over the past 25 years or so, I've noticed four common misconceptions regarding employees that many managers consider to be accurate. They accept that these misconceptions—I call them myths—are true and that nothing can be done to change the situation. And then they wonder why their employees' performance isn't as high as they'd like it to be. Consider the myths:

- All employees care about is getting a paycheck.
- Most employees don't care about improving their job performance.
- Employees understand exactly what is expected of them.
- Employees know exactly how well they're performing.

I am here to tell you that these myths are just that—myths. I'm not sure how they came to be held as truths, but by the time you've finished this chapter, you'll understand that, if you buy into the myths and figure you can't do anything to change employee behaviors, you're really inhibiting your employees and preventing them from being as productive and successful as possible.

Let's take a closer look at each of these myths.

They Only Want the Paycheck

Just like you and me, employees expect to be paid for their work, and, certainly, their paychecks are important to them. The paycheck, however, is not the sole motivation for most employees.

Study after study has shown, and I've personally witnessed, that factors other than monetary reward are important motivators for employees. If being paid were the sole motivation for employees, all you'd have to do is pay them and they'd do their very best work every day, right? You'd have a bunch of happy workers and never have to think twice about their performance levels, because they'd be working at top level in anticipation of their next check. As I'm sure you already know, that just isn't the way it works.

Factors such as job challenge, a supportive workplace, a degree of flexibility, recognition of achievement, value as a part of a team, a sense of investment in the goals and mission of the company, workplace fairness, and effective communication have been shown to be at least as motivating to employees as a paycheck. That's not to say that pay isn't important, but it's not the only reason employees work. You'll find further discussion about nonmonetary rewards in Chapter 18.

Once you set aside the myth that employees are in it only for the paycheck, you can concentrate on establishing or increasing other forms of motivation.

They Don't Care About the Job

Sure, an occasional employee is looking to slide by at work with as little effort as possible. Most workers, though, genuinely care about their jobs and want to perform them well. To do that, however, they need to feel invested in the work they're doing. They need to know how the work they do relates to the company and, more importantly, the customer.

PERFORMANCE GAP

Employee commitment—the bond or connection that employees feel to the company they work for—is largely dependent on the level of involvement in the company, loyalty employees feel toward the company, and the degree to which they feel invested in its goals and values. While managers can contribute to employee commitment, they can also damage it by being rigid, uncaring, and unresponsive to the needs of employees.

The majority of employees want to perform well in their jobs, but they need to be encouraged to do so, empowered to do so, and recognized and rewarded when they do.

They Know Exactly What You Expect

Managers often assume that employees understand what's expected of them, even when those expectations have never been expressed. Too often, employees are dropped into a job or an assignment and left to figure it out on their own. Then when they don't meet the expectations of the manager because they don't know what those expectations are, their work is viewed as poor.

This is a dilemma for both employees and managers. Many managers believe they've told employees what they expect of them, but they've stated their expectations in terms that are too vague or general to be of much use to employees. For instance, a manager might tell an employee that her job is to answer the phone, yet then complain that the employee isn't responding to calls the way the manager thinks she should. The employee, of course, was told only to answer the phone—not how the phone should be answered—and in her mind, she was fulfilling expectations.

Some managers buy into the thought that an employee who has received a job description should know exactly what the job entails and how it should be done. This is a dangerous assumption, considering the generic nature of most job descriptions. While a job description is a good start for expressing expectations, it's not a substitute for one-on-one communication and training.

PERFORMANCE BOOST

Employees are often reluctant to ask for more instruction or explanation of expectations, and managers too often assume that their workers know what is expected of them, even though they've never actually told them. Debunking this myth can save both employees and managers a lot of misunderstanding and frustration.

They Can Evaluate Their Own Performances

Every employee knows how well he or she is doing, right? Wrong. I've worked with many employees who were identified by their managers as poor performers yet thought they were doing just fine in their jobs. Why? Because nobody had ever told them they weren't achieving as well as they were expected to.

Without clearly defined expectations and feedback concerning job performance, the majority of employees don't know how well they're doing in their jobs. Most employees will assume, unless they're informed otherwise, that their work is okay—and many will assume that their work is good.

If you're dissatisfied with an employee's work performance, you're going to need to tell him. Lots of managers avoid that because it's uncomfortable or they don't want to hurt somebody's feelings. Understanding that it's your job to let employees know how they're doing, and to provide that feedback in a productive manner, will go a long way in boosting employee performance.

What Your Employees Need from You

An employer-employee or manager-employee relationship involves a lot of give-and-take. If the relationship is completely one sided, it's not going to work. A manager who must constantly make concessions to a disgruntled, complaining employee will soon tire of having to provide special treatment and will send the employee packing.

On the other hand, employees certainly won't respond well to, or strive to be as productive as possible for, a manager who isn't willing to consider their circumstances and needs or to meet them halfway on issues that matter.

More than anything, your employees need contact with you. They need to hear from you and know that you're accessible when they need you. They need effective communication so they know what's going on. They need to have a clear understanding of your expectations and be updated if those expectations change. Let's take a closer look at what you should be doing for your employees.

To Know What to Do

Have you ever been in a position where you simply didn't know what to do? Maybe you were in a new job, or maybe you came across an emergency situation you'd never encountered. The point is, not knowing what to do is an extremely uncomfortable position, and not one you want your employees to be in.

Managers sometimes fear that they'll appear to be condescending or too hands on by taking the time to walk through a job or assignment with an employee. They're afraid the employee will be offended if the manager pays too much attention to detail or relates too many expectations. After all, most employees have job descriptions. Isn't that enough?

The truth is, most employees want and need to know exactly what they are expected to do, and that takes more than a job description. Not understanding what they're supposed to do can make employees reluctant to do anything at all because they're afraid of making mistakes. If your employees seem to be unproductive, maybe they don't have a good understanding of what to do.

To Know How to Do It

You read the example earlier in this chapter of the employee who was told it was her job to answer the phone but was never informed of how she was to answer it. Cherie figured, and logically so, that the way she'd answered the phone at her previous job would be fine. So when she picked up the phone and said, "Miller, Clark, and Miller, how can I help you?" she figured she was meeting job expectations—after all, she was answering the phone, as instructed.

Cherie's boss, however, expected her to provide the caller with her full name, say either "good morning" or "good afternoon," and ask specifically how she could direct the call.

When the manager told Cherie she hadn't met job expectations in how she'd answered the phone, she was upset and frustrated. She wanted to perform her job well, but she couldn't know how to do that without being told. Once her boss talked to her and Cherie wrote out a little script, she turned out to be a great receptionist.

CASE IN POINT

One of my clients is a grocery store chain located in the Northeast. A manager was complaining one day that he'd asked an employee to clean out the walk-in cooler and the employee had done it all wrong. Upon further questioning, the manager admitted that he'd simply told the employee to clean out the cooler, not stated his expectations for how the cooler should be cleaned or what it should look like when the job was done. Had the manager told the employee up front how the job was to be done, the employee probably would have met—and perhaps exceeded—expectations.

It's true that some high-performing employees might prefer to be given an overview of a job and be left to figure it out on their own. Most workers, however, want to know not only what they're supposed to do, but how they're supposed to do it.

To Know Why They Need to Do It

I worked with a client whose employees produced cloth that was used to make curtains. Some employees had been making cloth for years and knew what it was used for, but had never seen the curtains that resulted from their efforts. When their employer arranged for them to visit a facility in which curtains made from their cloth were hanging, the employees finally got to see the results of their labors and understand why they performed the work they did. They were able to make the connection between their efforts and the results of those efforts. A big pride factor was involved, and the employees were excited and motivated.

Employees need to be able to see the bigger picture if they are to be motivated about their work. They need to be able to see the results of their efforts and understand why they do what they do. This spans nearly every field. Think about that for a minute.

A teacher surely desires to see results from his efforts, perhaps in a student who achieves higher test grades or gets admitted to a great college. A website designer no doubt is interested in whether her work results in increased traffic and business for her client. A worker in a manufacturing plant wants to understand how the small part he's responsible for fits into the larger machine that his company produces.

Workers who understand why they perform the work they do have a sense of purpose. If your employees aren't seeing the big picture that results from their efforts, it's up to you to help them understand.

To Know What They're Doing Right— and Wrong

As a manager, it's your job to provide feedback. Employees want and need to know what they're doing right and where they need to make improvements. Sure, you'll have the occasional worker who doesn't want to hear your advice or resents your suggestions, but most employees really want to clearly understand their strengths and weaknesses. They need you to help them do so.

You might have employees who understand their strengths and weaknesses in a general way, but not how they apply to the job they're responsible for. For instance, Julie might understand that, although she's a really good software engineer, her people skills aren't so great. She might not understand, however, that her difficult personality is dragging down the team she's been working with on an important special project, to the point that the project is in jeopardy. Julie has a general view of her strengths and weaknesses, but she doesn't realize how they are affecting the project she's been assigned to and the other people with whom she's working. It's your job as a manager to set Julie straight on her job performance and how it's affecting the project.

> **PERFORMANCE BOOST**
>
> Employees who don't receive appropriate feedback tend to assume that their performance is satisfactory and continue to perform the job in the same manner. This can result in a project getting off track or an employee inadvertently derailing the efforts of co-workers. Quickly addressing and dealing with unsatisfactory performance, however, can provide an opportunity to make changes to get back on track before it's too late.

Addressing strengths and weaknesses is not always easy, and, as you can imagine, it can result in hard feelings if not approached properly. You will learn much more about feedback in Chapter 6. For now, just understand that there are effective and ineffective ways of providing feedback to employees, but it's an important job and necessary for keeping workers motivated and productive.

Boosting Employee Performance Isn't Rocket Science

The truth is, on some level, you already know most of what you need to about boosting employee performance. You've either watched a good manager deal with employees or realized the tactics and behaviors that employees respond to during the course of your own career. You might end up being surprised at how much you already know.

Throughout this book, you'll learn about performance management and how it can help you motivate employees. You'll learn how to make sure employees know what's expected of them and how to monitor workers to make sure you always have a handle on how things are going. You'll get a better understanding of the importance of training, and you'll learn how to address performance issues with your employees as you coach them and give them feedback about how they're doing.

Boosting employee performance works best when engineered through a methodical process known as the performance management cycle. This proven process is effective in nearly every type of work environment, and it's easy to learn and implement. In fact, you've probably been practicing aspects of the performance management cycle—perhaps without even realizing it. If you're open to learning about the steps of the cycle and applying what you learn to your job, both you and your associates will benefit.

The Least You Need to Know

- Learn to think past employee myths and stereotypes.
- Employees want to know what to do, how to do it, and why they do it.
- Tell employees what they're doing right—and wrong.
- You know more than you think about boosting performance.

Get the Most from Your Employees

2

In This Chapter

- What is performance management?
- The four parts of the performance management cycle
- Setting new goals
- The center of performance management: customers and your organization's mission

You read in Chapter 1 that most employees really want to be invested in their jobs and perform their work to the best of their abilities. And you understand that, as a manager, it's your job to help them to do that. The question, then, is how can you take each of your employees to the next level? How do you help each one reach his or her full potential as an employee and, collectively, as a team?

The answer is to implement a performance management program that will boost performance and help your organization meet and exceed its goals.

In this chapter, you'll learn exactly what performance management is and how, when implemented and used properly, it can enhance individual and team performance while keeping every associate in tune with your organization's goals and values. Performance management doesn't require any specialized degrees or superhuman effort on your part—just a thorough understanding of how and why it works.

Understanding Performance Management

Performance management is the process of leading, developing, motivating, and evaluating the job performance of employees. The process is structured and systematic, and is set within a partnership relationship between employees and management. It's intended to improve communication between managers and employees, set standards and expectations, call out and address problems with performance, and recognize and reward good performance.

Basically, a performance management program involves four steps:

1. Establish job performance standards and expectations

2. Train

3. Coach

4. Provide effective performance reviews

Together, these four steps form a performance management cycle. The cycle is a closed-loop system in which the parts fit together, with each one dependent on the others. If you take away any one of the steps, the cycle falls apart; it works only with all four steps in place.

For example, what would happen if you set the standards and expectations, provided lots of coaching, and followed up with a performance review, but never bothered to make certain the employee was properly trained? You'd be setting up that employee to fail. The cycle simply can't work without all the steps.

At the center of the performance management cycle are your customers and the mission of your organization. Every step of the cycle should link employees to internal and external customers, as well as the mission.

PERFORMANCE BOOST

You need to think about how you'll implement performance management, and that takes some time. It's an ongoing, hands-on process. If you're serious about boosting employee performance, however, you've got to pay attention to performance management.

Step One: Establish Standards and Expectations

Most employees want to know and understand what is expected of them. And they want to know not only what they're supposed to do, but how they're supposed to do it. They also wonder how their performance will be measured.

Job performance standards and expectations provide all of that information for employees and help them to fully understand their purpose and goals. Simply put, a job performance standards and expectations statement is a verbal or written statement that tells an employee what to do, how to do it, how it will be measured, and how it links to the customer and the mission of the organization.

Your Employees Can't Read Your Mind

So, you might ask, what's the difference between a set of performance standards and expectations and a job description? Doesn't a job description tell an employee what's expected? While a typical job description does list duties pertaining to a particular position, the problem is that it doesn't include how or why the duty is to be performed, or how the employee's performance will be measured.

A job description might tell an employee that one of his job duties is to generate letters to applicants regarding the status of grants projects. It may not, however, specify that those letters must be mailed by 3 P.M. on the 15th of every month and that each one must contain certain information that is specific to a particular grant request. So if Jesse doesn't get his letters posted until 9 A.M. on the 16th, he hasn't fulfilled the expectations of his job. Why? Not because he didn't want to or wasn't willing to, but because he wasn't aware of or didn't understand the expectations.

My many years of experience working with clients has revealed that between 20 and 70 percent of employees don't boost their job performances because they don't understand what's expected of them. They want to be good workers and succeed and move forward in their jobs, but they can't because they simply don't have enough information about what they're supposed to be doing in order to perform at exceptional levels. Clearly stated job performance standards and expectations can remove that obstacle to success when employees truly understand them.

Give Them Goals That Make Sense

Goals are great when properly established and administered. Too often, however, goals are stated and either promptly forgotten or ignored, or referred to in vague and uncertain terms.

To be effective and useful, a goal must be clear, understandable, and measurable. There has to be a method of tracking progress toward the goal. It's great to set a goal of attaining 95 percent customer satisfaction for the coming year, but how are you going to know if you're on track for meeting that goal?

PERFORMANCE BOOST

Goals work best if they are SMART. That means they should be *specific, measurable, accountable, realistic,* and *timely.*

What steps are you going to take to improve performance to reach your goal? What level of customer satisfaction did you experience the previous year? Measurable goals are those such as, 50 percent of all employees will have completed customer service training by February 1, and 100 percent will have completed the training by April 1.

Goals that are vague and not easily measurable can be frustrating and confusing to employees—they're certainly not tools for boosting performance. Your job as a manager is to provide employees with task-oriented goals, not a general training directive that is difficult to figure out.

You can tell an employee that she is providing outstanding service to customers, but what does that mean? Until you tell her that outstanding service means greeting each customer who enters the store; asking how she can be of service; offering to hold items as the customer continues to shop; calling the customer by name, when possible; and thanking the customer, whether or not she buys something; your employee can't be expected to know what providing outstanding service looks like.

Communicate Clearly

You'll learn a lot about the importance of effective communication throughout this book, and it begins with being able to communicate job performance standards and expectations. To be able to meet standards and expectations, employees must first fully understand what they are. As a manager, you need to be an excellent communicator and make sure that you and your team members are on the same page.

Step Two: Provide Training

Training is vitally important and shouldn't be limited to just new employees. Job training must be ongoing and should be available to every employee. Many managers tend to assume that seasoned employees don't need any training because they understand the daily operations of the business.

What happens, though, when Brent gets moved from the stockroom to the sales floor, or Diedre gets promoted from sales associate to store manager? Both of them know the jobs they had been doing, but neither is experienced in the new job. Not providing training for the new jobs would put Brent and Diedre at high risk for failure.

Even experienced, successful employees require training when they take on new responsibilities or move to another job. New, inexperienced employees need even more training.

Training Techniques That Work

Training is simply any activity that's used to develop or improve skills, knowledge, or capabilities. The goal of training is to improve job performance and allow for employees to work with increased confidence and purpose. Training comes in many forms, ranging from sophisticated job simulations to self-study programs. One is not better than another, but some forms of training work better in particular circumstances and with particular employees than others.

Training is often viewed as an unessential expense when businesses are looking to trim their budgets. It's true that training can be expensive. It's also true that, in some organizations, employees are sent off for training that doesn't meet their specific needs or is based on ineffective techniques. While effective training is essential, what works varies from company to company. While some businesses stick with formal training programs, many small businesses find success with having a manager or another experienced employee train new employees or workers being moved to new positions. In any case, the use of training dollars should be carefully planned and implemented.

Not Everyone Learns the Same Way

You can't assume that every member of your team will benefit equally from the same types of training. Some people learn better when paired with other employees, while others do best with an online training program. Job shadowing—where an employee new to a company or position shadows an experienced employee to learn about the job he'll be performing—works for some employees, but other people are uncomfortable in that situation. A manager should never assume that a one-size-fits-all training program will work for all employees.

Here's an example. Cyndi, a registered nurse working for her county's Visiting Nurse Association, was meticulous about keeping records while in the field. She later transferred those records as Word documents onto her work PC. When Cyndi's supervisor told her that she would be responsible for filing her reports as Excel spreadsheets, Cyndi didn't know what to do. She'd never used Excel and had no interest in learning it. Her supervisor said she'd be given paid time to use the Excel tutorial to learn the program, but Cyndi was certain she wouldn't be able to understand it. Her colleague, Paul, on the other hand, was excited about the change and eager to learn the Excel program. He'd never used it, either, but he was certain he'd be able to pick it up quickly through the tutorial, which he did. Paul convinced Cyndi that the program wasn't difficult and offered to show her how to use it. They got permission for Paul to train Cyndi, and now both

RNs are happily creating spreadsheets. If Cyndi had been forced to learn the program from the tutorial, chances are, it would have taken her longer, she would have become frustrated, and perhaps her nursing work would have been impacted. Paul, on the other hand, jumped at the chance to use the tutorial and was then able to successfully pass along his knowledge to Cyndi.

Employees learn differently and have different comfort levels, and managers need to be adaptable and flexible when considering different types of training. What works for one employee may not work for all.

Keep Your Cool

If you've ever tried to learn something from a hurried and impatient teacher, you know that it can be a daunting and unproductive experience. Whether you're providing actual training for employees or just deciding what training is appropriate and setting it up, you'll find that employees respond much better to patient and realistic goals than to unrealistic ones. Sure, you need to lead, set boundaries, and establish expectations, but if your expectations are completely unrealistic or you insist on pushing someone ahead faster than he's able to go, employee performance will be negatively affected.

As a manager, your job is to inspire and help your employees to improve job performance. You'll be better able to achieve all those goals when you employ patience and maturity.

Step Three: Coaching Your Employees

Coaching—the act of providing feedback—is essential to boosting employee performance. Unfortunately, coaching is often overlooked. Coaching is anything you do or say that develops, reinforces, or improves the on-the-job performance of an employee. It's an integral part of the performance management cycle.

As with training, different team members respond more positively or negatively to various coaching styles, so you can't assume a one-size-fits-all approach.

When to Do It

Coaching must be practiced on an ongoing basis. Managers sometimes avoid coaching because they don't want to appear overly critical or look like they're checking up on employees. A worker who doesn't get any feedback, however, will assume that everything is going well, even if it isn't.

CASE IN POINT

Ross had been employed for almost a year as a reporter for a midsize city newspaper. Ross loved his job, and whenever anyone asked him how it was going, he would enthusiastically talk about how great it was. After all, with little feedback from his supervisor, Ross had no reason to believe anything was wrong. As a result, he was shocked when his supervisor told him at his performance review that he hadn't been happy with Ross's performance for most of his employment. The supervisor should have been working with Ross all along, offering feedback and working with him to take steps to improve his performance, instead of letting Ross assume that everything was okay.

An employee who is alerted to performance problems through coaching has the opportunity to work to improve performance. One who isn't alerted, however, probably will continue to underachieve due to a lack of awareness of the problem. Coaching cannot be a once-in-a-while effort or be provided only once a year during a performance review; it needs to be practiced on a predictable and ongoing basis.

How to Do It

Feedback can be provided in different ways. If you're like most people, you're probably pretty comfortable with offering supportive feedback, which encourages and bolsters. That sort of feedback is important and should be used regularly. You might, however, be less comfortable with offering corrective or evaluative feedback, which can be difficult to give and receive.

Regardless of the sort of feedback you're offering, you can take steps to make sure it's effective and productive. For example, you can make sure the feedback is based on performance; is offered in a timely manner; and is specific, nonjudgmental, and based on fact. You'll learn more about effective feedback in Part 2.

> **PERFORMANCE GAP**
>
> Managers sometimes have trouble understanding the difference between training and coaching, and often lump the two together. However, these are different processes with different purposes. The purpose of training is to pass on knowledge, whereas coaching is used to provide feedback on performance.

Coaching Moments

Managers sometimes assume an "if it's not broken, don't fix it" approach to coaching. Certainly, as in the case of Ross, performance problems should be addressed promptly and in an ongoing manner. However, coaching should not be limited to cases of performance problems. Key coaching moments—opportunities to offer feedback and help—arise in four different situations:

- When an associate meets your expectations
- When an associate exceeds your expectations
- When there is a gap in performance
- During the performance review meeting

Coaching in all of these situations keeps you in tune with your team and establishes you as a partner, not just a supervisor. This builds trust, which is essential in helping your employees boost their performance.

Step Four: Provide Feedback

The final step of the performance management cycle is the performance review. This may not be your favorite piece of the management pie, but smart managers will make sure that the review is as productive and positive as it can be.

A performance review not only serves as a tool to review past performance, but it also provides an opportunity for an employee and manager to work together to establish expectations for the coming year.

Be Thorough

Once you've completed the first three steps of the performance management cycle, a performance review shouldn't seem like such a big deal. Reviews often get blown out of proportion and are dreaded by both managers and employees, but that doesn't need to be the case.

Employees who fully understand performance expectations and standards, and have been properly trained and coached throughout the year, won't be in for a lot of surprises during performance reviews. They'll already know whether they've met or exceeded expectations, and if there's been a performance gap—a difference between the expected level of performance and the actual level of performance—you and they will have already addressed it.

Your role is to look at the overall cycle and address all of its parts. You review job performance standards and expectations, and discuss whether any changes are necessary. You determine whether additional training is called for and use your coaching notes to review conversations and actions regarding job performance that occurred before the review.

The review simply serves as an opportunity for the two of you to engage in an in-depth discussion, which serves to maintain positive performance. It also is an opportunity to enhance a positive working relationship with a particular employee and to start off the next performance management cycle on a high note.

PERFORMANCE GAP

Avoid any temptation to overlook or sugarcoat a problem during a performance review. A problem that isn't addressed doesn't disappear; it simply remains as an unaddressed problem.

Keep It Positive, Fair, and Factual

It's important to be prepared when you go into a performance review and to make sure you're comfortable with the key points to be discussed. The review should focus both on positive aspects of performance and on any areas in which improvement may be necessary. Make sure you have coaching notes to support whatever conversation is necessary, and resolve to maintain a positive and upbeat attitude throughout the review.

Performance reviews are generally the arena for discussing pay increase or bonus recommendations. Because of this (and other reasons), they can potentially become emotionally charged. Whatever you do, do not allow the discussion to become personal. Stick to the facts, be as fair as you can, and document all discussion by making notes during the meeting and drafting them into a memo following the review. Documentation is extremely important so that you will remember what occurred and a record of the meeting will be available in the event that anyone else needs to see it.

Involve the Employee

A performance review is a great opportunity to foster personal development in employees. Ask about employees' career plans and how they hope to advance within the organization. Discuss whether they're interested in receiving more training or in learning about another aspect of the job. Employees who know that their supervisors are genuinely interested in them and want them to succeed respond positively, take more ownership of their jobs, and become more productive and higher-performing employees. Encourage her to share any concerns or questions that she has, and, if you don't have answers at the moment, make notes to follow up, and make sure to follow through.

Close the Cycle

The performance review is the final step in the performance management cycle, but new goals must be set in order for the cycle to close. A discussion on goals for the coming year might be part of the review process, or it may be a follow-up to the performance review.

Setting new goals serves as a starting point for defining expectations and setting job performance standards for the coming year. If standards and expectations will be different, it's your job to let the employee know exactly how and why. It's a good idea to follow up on a performance review to reinforce discussion and make sure you and the employee are on the same page. You can do this by drafting a memo following the review, outlining what occurred, and suggesting a date for a follow-up meeting to discuss whether goals are being met. Be sure to have your employee confirm the date of the meeting and mark your calendar to ensure that it will happen.

Remember Who You're Working For

The performance management cycle outlines what you, as a manager, need to accomplish to boost employee performance and help employees achieve their greatest potentials. While the steps of the cycle are action oriented and interdependent of one another, it's important to remember what all the steps are directed toward.

CASE IN POINT

A long-time client has a company with the mission "We will Exceed Your Needs." That statement shapes the expectations of employees, managers, and customers, and drives everything the company does. The company manufactures equipment that must be delivered to customers in a "just in time" environment—that is, at exactly the time the customer is ready to use it. Getting materials delivered on time is crucial because the customer can't operate without them. Everything related to performance management within this company is based on how well it achieves its stated goal of exceeding the needs of its customers. The company's training, expectations, coaching, and performance reviews all link back to its mission statement, which directs employees to deliver not only on time, but ahead of time.

If customers and your organization's mission aren't firmly in place as the centerpiece of the cycle, the cycle will collapse. Everything you and your employees do, from establishing job performance standards and expectations to holding the performance review, must point to your customers and your mission.

The Least You Need to Know

- Performance management boosts performance and helps your organization meet and exceed its goals.
- The four steps of the performance management cycle are to establish job performance standards and expectations, train, coach, and review performance.
- Each step of the cycle is necessary and dependent on the others.
- Your organization's mission and its customers must remain at the center of the performance management cycle.

Define Standards and Expectations

In This Chapter

- Empowering employees to succeed
- Defining levels of performance
- Measuring job performance
- Using the tools for assessing performance

You've read that employees want to know what they're supposed to do and how they're supposed to do it. You've also read that, although job postings and descriptions can serve as starting points, they generally include only the *what*, not the *how*. Job descriptions do a good job of informing employees on the major tasks they're expected to perform, but not so much on how to perform them. They don't tell employees how to successfully accomplish those tasks or what the results of their efforts should look like.

That's not to say that job descriptions are not important or can't be valuable tools, particularly if you take the time to review them periodically with employees. Job descriptions have limits, however, and that's why it's necessary to define expectations and standards for each major job duty. That simply means adding the *how*, and perhaps a *why*, to the *what*.

You can't expect to boost employee performance until you're certain that employees understand what you expect that performance to include. A lack of understanding of performance expectations and standards is a primary cause of performance gaps. Fortunately, it's an easy problem to fix.

Beyond the Job Description

Take a look at this job description for a mechanic who works in a public school district.

Overview: Perform a wide variety of technical repairs to school vehicles and equipment.

Job Responsibilities:

- Maintain and recondition diesel and gasoline engines
- Make minor body and suspension repairs
- Repair and maintain pneumatic, electrical, and hydraulic systems on busses and other motor vehicles
- Mount tires; weld broken components; adjust and repair brakes, lights, and other accessories on district vehicles
- Conduct safety inspections on district vehicles
- Act as substitute driver, as required
- Perform other duties, as required

Although the job description lists major duties, thereby telling the employee what to do, it offers no clue to how the tasks are to be performed. For instance, what's entailed in conducting a safety inspection on a district vehicle? Is it a visual inspection? Does the vehicle need to be put on a lift? Do tires need to be rotated?

What's involved in serving as a substitute driver? What time does the driver need to be available to start the route? How will the substitute know the route? In what condition does the bus need to be returned to the depot?

PERFORMANCE GAP

On their own, job descriptions can actually be limiting. You've heard the line "Sorry, that's not in my job description," right? Unmotivated employees who aren't interested in boosting performance or advancing their employment status could actually use their job descriptions to try to limit their responsibilities.

A job description for an administrative assistant includes tasks such as making sure the office is kept in an orderly and clean fashion and maintaining inventory for office supplies and computer software.

Again, while the description tells the administrative assistant what to do, it offers no advice on how to do it and doesn't provide a picture of the results. What are the characteristics of an orderly and clean office, for example? Is it the job of the administrative assistant to empty trash cans or tidy up desks? What does it mean to maintain inventory? Does that mean all supplies are to be fully stocked, or should they be reordered when the stock gets below 50 percent?

While a job description lists duties, an explanation of expectations and standards tells employees how a job is to be performed and sets the standards to which job performance is measured. Merely establishing and communicating expectations helps boost performance by ensuring that you and your employees have the same expectations and understanding of what needs to be accomplished and in what manner.

Defining Expectations

Performance expectations should be stated in clear and specific terms that tell employees what they are to do and how, or to what standard the job task should be performed. If an employee or job task is new, the purpose of the task also should be explained. Employees need to know why they're doing what they're doing.

Keep the following questions in mind when establishing performance standards and expectations. They can help you cover all the bases and let employees know exactly the standards to which they're expected to perform:

- What will a good job look like?
- How is an employee expected to behave when performing a task?
- How long should it take to complete a job?
- What is an employee expected to produce within that time?

- How can the job be performed in a safe manner?

- How can the job be performed in an economical manner?

- What job results are considered satisfactory?

- What job results are considered exemplary?

- Do any company or other rules or regulations affect how the job should be performed?

Stating your job performance expectations in the context of these questions will ensure that you've explained not only what is to be done, but how. The following examples illustrate the difference between telling somebody what to do and establishing expectations for how it should be done.

Ryan's job is to clean out the walk-in cooler in the grocery store where he works. Ryan's manager tells him to clean the cooler, and Ryan sets about performing the task. Because Ryan has no idea what his manager expects, he cleans the cooler in a way that seems reasonable to him, but he does not meet the (unexpressed) expectation of his manager. As a result, the manager is unhappy, Ryan gets chewed out because he hasn't properly cleaned the cooler, and Ryan has to repeat the task.

If, on the other hand, the manager had told Ryan that he was to clean out the cooler by pulling out all products, washing and disinfecting every surface, and returning the products to the cooler with the nearest expiration dates at the front, Ryan would have known exactly what was expected and how to accomplish the task.

In addition, if the manager had told him that the purpose of cleaning the cooler is to ensure sanitation, keep the stock fresh, and provide the best possible service to the customer, Ryan would have understood why he was performing the task and probably would have felt invested in his work.

PERFORMANCE BOOST

Performance expectations need to describe anticipated results of the job, as well as the activities to be performed during the job.

Deanna is a medical technician who performs echocardiograms, a type of ultrasound, on cardiac patients. Deanna knows well how to perform the medical procedure, but her supervisor was unhappy with the manner in which she treated patients. She felt that Deanna wasn't providing the sort of personal service on which the practice prided itself.

Once the supervisor established and clearly expressed the performance expectations and standards to Deanna, however, Deanna understood that she needed to walk out to the waiting room and greet each patient by name, then escort the patient to the room in which the echocardiogram was to be performed, explain how the procedure would be done, and ask whether the patient had any questions.

Deanna was completing the tests just fine, but she didn't understand that the purpose of giving each patient personal attention and service was to provide a comfortable environment for patients who were likely to be stressed out over being there in the first place.

As a manager, you need to both establish specific and measurable expectations and then keep those expectations in mind so that you can assess how your employees are performing.

What's Okay?

Employees who meet the established expectations are doing okay. They're not setting the world on fire, but they're performing up to the level that's expected of them.

The office worker who always answers the phone by the third ring, as expected, is doing okay—just fine, in fact. The customer service representative who makes sure he gets back to a customer about a question within an hour, as he's expected to do, is meeting expectations. Your challenge with employees who meet expectations, of course, is to boost their performance to the next level.

What's Better Than Okay?

Exceeding expectations is better than okay. It's better than good—it's excellent performance. This is the employee who not only gets back to a customer with an answer to a question, but goes above and beyond the call of duty to track an order, locate an item from a different location, or answer the phone every time by the second ring instead of the third. An employee who exceeds expectations makes 30 widgets an hour instead of 25, or figures out a new system for keeping the freezer organized and helps to implement it.

Managers need to first recognize these employees, value them, and work to keep them motivated in order to boost their performance even further.

What Just Doesn't Cut It?

If you've been a manager for a while, you've likely had to deal with performance gaps. Gaps occur when an employee doesn't meet the expectations that have been established. The phone rings five times, the mail doesn't get delivered until after lunch, or a customer's phone call is not returned for two days instead of the expected one hour.

Performance gaps occur for various reasons, and your job as a manager is to figure out which applies to your employee and how to address and correct the problem.

 PERFORMANCE GAP

Don't assume that you know why a performance gap is occurring. There are lots of reasons why gaps occur, and it's a mistake to rush into trying to fix a problem before you know what's causing it.

How to Measure Performance

A sales associate might be expected to serve 15 customers every hour. That's a quantitative and very measurable performance standard. He is also expected to provide that service in a pleasant and effective manner. Those expectations are qualitative or observable.

To effectively measure an employee's performance, you have to address the whole picture. It doesn't matter that Steve serves 20 customers an hour if he behaves rudely and belittles them as he does so. Let's look at some common ways of measuring performance—quality, quantity, and time—and how the methods often overlap.

Quality

Quality often is harder to measure than quantity or time because it's more subjective. What's good quality to one person may not be good to another. As a supervisor, you can't just tell employees that their work isn't good enough—you need to tell them why it isn't and how they can make sure they get it right the next time. Employees also need to understand how the quality of their work is measured. Some criteria for measuring the quality of work include the following:

- Customer satisfaction
- Number of complaints in connection to job performance
- Percentage of work output that must be redone
- Peer perceptions of job performance
- Adherence to safety standards
- Adherence to procedure
- Work completed within budget
- Manner of behavior of employee
- Percentage of leads that result in sales
- Consistency of work quality

Megan, a graphic designer, produced a postcard advertising a meditative retreat for a client who owns a holistic health center. Megan was really pleased with her work and was eager to show it to her boss, Tom, and to the client.

Tom, however, wasn't happy with the job and told Megan so. Megan got very defensive and upset, until Tom took the time to sit down with her and explain that the text was placed differently than the client had requested, and the colors were quite a bit brighter than they'd discussed. Tom knew this client well and could anticipate that she wouldn't be happy with the work because she prefers muted color tones and doesn't like when her suggestions for placing text aren't followed exactly.

Megan had finished the job on time and adhered to the specifications for size, how many to print, and so forth, but she hadn't met the expectations of the client, which surely would have resulted in a complaint had Tom not intervened and made sure the job was redone.

Measuring the quality of job performance often requires judgment calls, but having criteria in place can clarify expectations for everyone.

Quantity

Measuring job performance in terms of quantity is much more cut and dried than using quality as a measure, although some variables might still be in play. You can measure the number of sales calls made in a day or the number of units produced on a manufacturing line. The number of hours worked that can be billed to a client can be an indicator of job performance, as can the number of applications filed, reports typed, or shirts folded.

Be aware, however, that a sales associate who knows that the number of calls he makes each day is an indicator of his job performance might change his routine or technique in order to achieve a greater number of calls. That might be a good thing, but it could cause problems.

If Carl is the best salesperson you have because he's pleasant and always takes time to not only thoroughly explain the service you're selling, but create goodwill by asking customers about their families, then cutting short his phone time in order to increase the number of calls could actually result in fewer sales. In similar cases, shirts could end up sloppily folded or reports could be not completed to specification. While quantity often is a dependable indicator of job performance, it always should be used in conjunction with qualitative measurement. It's great if your workers increase their productivity by turning out a thousand extra units per week, but not at the expense of worker safety or employee morale.

CASE IN POINT

Carly was the best flower designer in the shop, and the fastest. On busy days, she could turn out one arrangement after another, always to the satisfaction of customers. Her attitude, however, was far below her design abilities, and other employees had an extremely difficult time getting along with her. She wasn't permitted to deal directly with customers because her interpersonal skills were so poor, which meant that other designers had to pick up her slack when it came to answering phones or taking orders. While Carly's performance was excellent when measured by the floral arrangements she turned out, her overall performance fell short.

Measuring job performance solely on the basis of quantity can be problematic and usually is more effective when combined with another measure. In some cases, however, quantity is a fair and accurate way in which to measure performance.

Time

Time comes into play in many areas of job performance and is another easily measured factor. Was the product delivered by 3 P.M. on Thursday, as promised? Was the December 15 project deadline met? Was fresh coffee brewed every 20 minutes? Was every customer greeted within two minutes of entering the store?

As with quantity, however, using time as your only means of measuring performance can be problematic. If a customer dropped a pot of coffee onto the floor while pouring a takeout order, chances are, an associate might be busy assisting with cleanup when it's time to brew a fresh pot. If the product wasn't delivered by 3 P.M. on Thursday because there was a major hurricane that day, time isn't a good indicator of performance. However, the time factor paired with quality and quantity performance expectations can help you measure how your employees perform.

Troubleshooting Poor Performance

Employees who don't meet job performance expectations generally fail to do so because of four reasons. If employees don't meet or exceed job expectations, the first thing you'll need to do is spend some time observing and talking with them to determine what's going on.

Chances are, you'll discover that their performance gaps can be attributed to one or more of the following causes:

- They don't know what's expected of them.
- They don't know how to perform the job.
- They aren't capable of performing the job.
- They don't want to do the job.

Consider Megan, the graphic designer mentioned earlier. It could be that Megan doesn't understand that her primary job is to please the client, not to produce a postcard that she thinks looks great but isn't what the client wanted. This could have happened because she didn't understand the job expectations, or she isn't grasping the concept that the customer is at the center of the performance management cycle.

Or maybe Ryan missed some training time because he was out sick for a few days and never learned the procedure for cleaning out the cooler. If that's the case, he simply needs to be told how to perform the job. It's not that he doesn't want to perform his job properly or can't be easily taught to do it; he just doesn't know how to.

Employees who aren't capable of performing a job can be problematic. You need to figure out why they're unable to do it and then determine whether additional training would resolve the matter. If a physical condition is causing the problem, you might address whether accommodations could be made. If an employee is unable to do the job because he or she is incapable of learning how to do it, you'll need to think about moving the employee to a different assignment or hiring someone else.

PERFORMANCE GAP

Keeping an incompetent or unwilling employee can negatively affect other team members, who may become resentful if they perceive that an employee is not being held accountable for his or her actions. Over time, members of your team will lose respect for you, and you'll risk losing control of your employees.

Some employees experience performance gaps because they just don't want to perform a particular task. Sometimes there's a legitimate reason for that. For example, it may be Tonya's job to make at least eight pots of coffee every hour, but the smell of coffee makes her sick. Other times, an attitude problem may require action on your part.

Be aware that these problems sometimes overlap and occur together. Ryan may lack an understanding of his job expectations and also missed the training on how to clean the cooler. Megan may not have the skills necessary to visualize the client's wishes for her postcard and also may not realize the importance of keeping the client at the center of the performance cycle.

Nobody said that being a manager is always a walk in the park, and troubleshooting poor performance is one of those incidences when you need to be discerning, employ good people skills, and use appropriate action to address and correct the problems.

Connecting Performance Expectations and Reviews

As you establish performance expectations, be sure employees understand that they are directly linked to the performance reviews in their futures. Job performance expectations and the performance review forms used during performance reviews should work hand in hand, with the expectations and goals serving as the basis for the performance review form.

Too often, performance review forms aren't linked to job expectations, and that makes no sense. If you never tell Bob in the accounting department that, in addition to his analytical skills, he'll be evaluated on teamwork and his ability to get along with co-workers, he's going to be in for a big surprise when he learns of those expectations during his performance review. It's like a teacher handing out a test on which the questions have nothing to do with the information in the book students were advised to study. In short, it's not fair.

PERFORMANCE GAP

Employees who show up to a performance review and find out they've been evaluated in areas they never knew about, typically feel angry and resentful. Understandably, this can seriously damage a manager/employee relationship and is in no way conducive to boosting performance.

A performance review form is a scorecard. And just like the card you keep as you advance through a round of golf, the form should be filled in as the performance review cycle moves along.

New employees should see the form the first day they're on the job, at the same time the job expectations are laid out. You also should periodically review performance review forms with established employees, as expectations may change. Some employers post performance review forms on bulletins boards for the entire department to see and review. This helps get everyone on the same page for both performance expectations and the way in which they'll be evaluated, which can help avoid suspicion and fear concerning the performance review process.

Performance reviews vary, of course, based on position and organization. Employees can be evaluated in these categories, among others:

- Job knowledge
- Safety
- Quality of work
- Teamwork
- Communication
- Customer service
- Ability to meet goals
- Leadership

- Flexibility

- IT/equipment/machinery skills

- Time management

Make sure you include all categories in which your employees will be rated, and update the performance review form as needed between performance reviews. The following sample form is used by a chain of retail grocery stores. Remember that it's just a sample—you'll have to customize it for your use. Make sure you include all categories in which your employees will be rated, and update the performance review form as needed between performance reviews.

PERFORMANCE REVIEW FORM

Date: _____   Store #: _____

Associate: _____

Position: _____   Hire date: _____

Reviewing manager: _____

Employees will be evaluated on the effectiveness of their performance by comparing it to the company's performance standard. For each characteristic, check the box next to the description that best fits the associate.

1. KNOWLEDGE OF WORK
Understanding of all phases of work and related aspects of associate's position

- ❑ Exceeds standards: Well informed; possesses thorough knowledge of all aspects of the position
- ❑ Meets standards: Adequate knowledge of all aspects of the position
- ❑ Below standards: Limited knowledge of the position

continues

---

continued

2. QUALITY OF WORK
Thoroughness, neatness, and efficiency of work

❑ Exceeds standards: Better-than-average work; very few errors; consistent performer

❑ Meets standards: Work performance standard in most instances

❑ Below standards: Work performance below standard in some or all areas

3. WORK PRODUCTIVITY
Quantity of acceptable work during established time frame

❑ Exceeds standards: Consistently completes assigned tasks and handles other responsibilities as well

❑ Meets standards: Consistently completes assigned tasks

❑ Below standards: Does not complete assigned tasks within established time frames

4. ATTENDANCE AND PUNCTUALITY
Consistent timeliness with all aspects of the time and attendance program

❑ Exceeds standards: No time and attendance violations; flexible in scheduling

❑ Meets standards: Attendance and punctuality are adequate, notifies when necessary; limited time and attendance violations

❑ Below standards: Moderately dependable; some time and attendance violations

5. FOLLOW-THROUGH
Extent to which employee can be counted on to complete assigned tasks

❑ Exceeds standards: Addresses tasks and issues needing follow-through; requires only occasional supervision

❑ Meets standards: Addresses most tasks and issues needing follow-through; requires some supervision

❑ Below standards: Needs more supervision than others on some work; not fully dependable on follow-through

6. ASSOCIATE RELATIONS
Ability to work harmoniously and effectively with fellow associates

- ❑ Exceeds standards: Has positive, good relationships with fellow employees; cooperative
- ❑ Meets standards: Maintains satisfactory relationships with fellow employees; generally cooperative
- ❑ Below standards: Relationships with fellow employees are fair; cooperates at times

7. CUSTOMER RELATIONS
Ability to provide courteous, friendly, and respectful service

- ❑ Exceeds standards: Ensures very strong customer relations
- ❑ Meets standards: Generally provides good customer relations
- ❑ Below standards: Occasionally considers and meets customers' needs

8. CHECK APPROPRIATE BOX INDICATING OVERALL JOB PERFORMANCE

- ❑ Exceeds standards
- ❑ Meets standards
- ❑ Below standards

If you're drafting a performance review form to share with your employees, remember to closely consult the job performance expectations you've established for them and connect the two, with the expectations forming the basis for the approval.

The Least You Need to Know

- Well-defined job expectations tell an employee what to do, how to do it, and why to do it.
- Defined standards must be in place to measure performance.
- Common measures of performance are quality, quantity, and time.
- Performance gaps generally can be attributed to lack of understanding, lack of knowledge, lack of ability, or lack of desire to perform a job.
- Performance expectations form the basis for performance review forms.

Keys to Clear Communication

In This Chapter

- Hurdles in making your expectations understood
- Using receipt of communication to ensure understanding
- Assessing your communication skills
- Recognizing circumstances that demand excellent communication

Establishing comprehensive job performance standards and expectations is important, but if you can't, or don't, communicate them to your employees, they are useless. Employees aren't mind readers, although managers sometimes seem to forget that.

Communicating at work is such an important topic that entire books have been written about it. Good communication is key to good management. If you can't communicate your expectations to your team, you can't expect for them to be met, much less exceeded.

In this chapter, you'll learn some effective methods for communicating with your employees and making sure that they fully understand what you're saying.

Don't Assume That Everyone Gets It

You probably assume that, when you tell somebody something, they know what you're saying, right? They get it. If you lay out job performance expectations to your employees, they're going to understand them and everything will be fine. Well, maybe. Then again, maybe not.

It's a fact that people hear and interpret information differently. You can tell two people the exact same piece of information, and they may interpret it in two completely different manners. This happens for a variety of reasons:

- **Varying frames of reference.** Someone who has worked for many years may grasp a manager's expectations more clearly than a new worker because that employee has accrued a variety of work experience under the leadership of different managers.

- **Listening skills.** Listening is indeed a skill, and workers who practice effective listening tend to comprehend instructions and information more effectively than those who don't.

- **Personal variables such as emotional state or prejudice.** Something said to someone who is agitated or upset might be interpreted differently than if that person is calm and relaxed.

- **Communication style of person relating information.** Some managers like to present a lot of background information when introducing an idea or stating expectations, while others get right to the point. Some speak slowly and deliberately, while others speak quickly and casually. Employees respond differently to various communication styles.

- **Type of information related.** If you're relating some very technical information or expectations that involve a lot of technical jargon, the members of your team who are more technologically savvy will have an easier time understanding you than those who aren't. The nontechies in your group may actually tune you out because they don't get what you're saying.

As a result of these and other variables, you can express the same expectations to a group of three people, or to each individual, but you can't expect everyone who hears you to end up with the same understanding.

Worse yet, each of the three team members might think that he or she heard and correctly understood the expectations expressed, thereby feeling no need to ask you to repeat or clarify them. Many managers then assume that their employees actually do have a clear understanding of the expectations and are surprised when performance gaps occur.

To avoid that unpleasant surprise and ensure that your employees are equipped to do their best and boost their job performances, you need to be absolutely sure that your expectations are understood—by everyone. The following example gives you an idea of what can happen when employees don't have the same expectations about a job.

Lee manages a team of technicians at a midsize information technology (IT) company. During the past few months, he's received a series of complaints from the company's sales force that the online sales manual they depend on is hard to understand and cumbersome to use. So Lee puts the word out to his team that the manual needs to be revised to make it more user-friendly. One team member immediately assumed that the manual needed to be completely overhauled and wasn't at all happy about it. Another figured that she could just rearrange some of the content to make the manual easier to use—no big deal. The third team member interpreted Lee's instruction as Lee had imagined: that flow diagrams should be incorporated into the manual to better illustrate the procedures. Each of the three technicians made valid interpretations, based on Lee's vague instruction to make the manual more user-friendly. Lee should have stated his expectations, of course, by telling his team that, before the sales conference on March 1, they had to make the manual more user-friendly by inserting flow diagrams and defining all terms that were not already explained. Stating his expectations at the onset of the project would have saved Lee and his team members time and aggravation.

Using Receipt of Communication

Once you've clearly expressed your expectations to members of your team, you need to ask them to step up and tell you what you said. Some managers aren't comfortable with having employees interpret information back to them because they're afraid it will seem condescending or put workers on the spot. I understand that you don't want to come off as being overbearing or heavy-handed, but this is a recognized technique that's proven to work, and it can help you avoid a lot of problems.

The technique is called receipt of communication, or ROC, and it's a method that's used to clarify understanding by having a person who listened to an instruction restate the instruction to the person who related it. As the employee is reiterating what's been said, you should be able to get an idea of whether he understands the instruction. If he sounds hesitant, be sure to ask if he has any questions. ROC is simply a means of making sure that you and your employee are both on the same page. I've found that, once you explain to your employees the purpose of using ROC, they generally don't mind playing along.

Why You Need to Do This

You need to use ROC because it benefits everyone on your team. You benefit because you can be sure that your expectations are understood. Your employees benefit because they'll know exactly what they're supposed to do, how to do it, and why they're doing it. They'll have the tools they need in order to boost their performances and be successful in their jobs.

Asking for ROC is easy and useful, and it's one of the easiest means of preventing misunderstandings that can result in performance gaps and affect your entire department.

Asking questions such as the following will help you achieve ROC regarding your expectations for employees. Their answers to such questions will let you know whether they are on board with what a job requires and how they will perform it. Take a couple minutes to think of some questions you might ask your employees:

- "Alex, tell me how you plan to …."

- "Jennifer, how can we get this done by end of shift? Any suggestions?"

- "Jason, just to be sure I have given you all the information you need to set up the display, could you please review what needs to be done?"

- "Margaret, tell me what you will do if …."

- "Anthony, just to be sure we are both on the same page, why don't you review with me how you plan to do this."

- "Joanne, how do you think we could get this job done more quickly?"

- "Ali, what do you think is the best way we can do this?"

The number of workplace problems, ranging from hurt feelings to dire safety issues, that could be avoided through effective communication is astounding, and I'm still surprised at the number of managers who are reluctant to embrace an easy means of improving communication with their employees.

Sure, the process of ROC takes a little time, especially when you and your team members are just starting to use it. Once it becomes second nature, however, you'll wonder how you ever managed without it.

Clarifying Your Expectations

Parents frequently complain that kids and teenagers have selective hearing, or no hearing, or that they tell you one thing and end up doing another. I've often thought that if parents used ROC with their kids, it might have the same benefits it has with employees.

You can ask your employees (or your kids) some questions to help you achieve ROC. They're simply questions that encourage employees to talk about the task or work they're planning to perform; their answers provide insight on their understanding of the job. Before asking these questions, you need to have thoroughly explained the job and expressed your expectations for how it should be done.

ROC is an underused technique, but it's definitely a win-win proposition for employees and managers. If you haven't tried it, you should.

Write It Down

A really effective means of communicating at work is putting your job performance expectations in writing for your employees and having them provide written ROC.

Saying it is good, but writing is better because it's more permanent and can be reviewed repeatedly, as needed. Just as employees have written job descriptions, they should have written versions of job performance expectations and should be encouraged to refer to them often.

> **PERFORMANCE BOOST**
>
> Writing job performance expectations not only gets them on a screen or paper to be checked and reviewed as needed, but the act of writing them reinforces the knowledge and understanding of the expectations. That's a good thing!

Having team members reiterate performance expectations to you in writing gives you a concrete feel for what they're thinking and planning, and how you might continue to be helpful in moving them forward.

How Well Do You Communicate?

Effective communication within a workplace goes beyond just passing along information. It facilitates healthy exchange of ideas and opinions, encourages creativity, fosters relationships, and provides the opportunity for resolving issues or solving problems. Yet in many organizations, communication is ineffective or even lacking. Many companies still talk around issues or exclude employees from discussion.

As you know, the manner in which we communicate has changed drastically in the past decade or so, with increased opportunities for communicating anywhere, at any time. Typed memos and notes on bulletin boards, formerly mainstays of intercompany communication, have given way to e-mails, webinars, tweets, and text messages. How many times do you e-mail someone within your office or building from your desk instead of delivering the information in person?

Electronic communication is efficient and extremely useful, but it's not a substitute for one-on-one communication between managers and employees. Believe me, there's a big difference between workplaces that value and employ personal communication and those that don't. That's not to say you should get rid of your BlackBerry, but don't be tempted to use it as a permanent substitute for other means of communication.

PERFORMANCE GAP

Even if you prefer to communicate with your employees by e-mail or text messaging, certain types of information should never, except in very extreme cases, be delivered in any manner other than in person. Never communicate layoffs or pay cuts through e-mail, and never, ever, electronically notify an employee of a termination. Those are surefire methods for losing the respect of your team.

You can spend a lot of time and money learning how to communicate effectively with your employees. Often, however, just making an effort to be aware of how you communicate can improve the way you relate to employees. Take a few minutes to complete the following quiz. It will give you an idea of how well you communicate and make you aware of areas in which you might need some improvement.

Quiz: Assess Your Communication Skills

Think about how you interact daily with others at work. Read each statement carefully and rate yourself as one of the following:

1 Never

2 Infrequently

3 Sometimes

4 Usually

5 Always

You may also want to ask a colleague to rate you in these areas. You might be surprised to find out that your colleague's impressions of your communication skills vary from your own.

1. I give my full attention to others when they are speaking. _____

2. I ask questions to help get clarification. _____

3. I paraphrase what others say to get "shared understanding." _____

4. People understand my instructions or requests for information. _____

5. I maintain good eye contact during a conversation. _____

6. People tell me I'm an effective speaker. _____

7. I show respect to others when they are speaking. _____

8. I notice and am sensitive to another person's nonverbal communication. _____

9. I speak up at team or department meetings. _____

10. I try to empathize with others' points of view. _____

11. I adjust my communication style to the needs of the individual or group. _____

12. I freely express my feelings to others. _____

13. I encourage further contribution from others during a discussion. _____

14. I'm aware of my nonverbal communication methods and use them effectively. _____

15. I give instructions that are clear and specific. _____

16. I refrain from using sarcasm when making a point. _____

17. I enjoy making presentations. _____

18. People compliment me on my verbal communication skills. _____

19. People ask my advice on how they could be more effective communicators. _____

20. I consider carefully the best way to package my message. _____

Add up your total score: _____

Now let's see how well you did.

90–100: Congratulations! You are an excellent communicator. Keep on doing what you're doing.

80–89: Your communication skills are good, but you may need to work harder in certain areas. Review your answers and take special note of your "3" ratings.

79 or below: The bad news is that your communication skills are in need of repair. The good news is that you can improve them by being aware of the areas in which you're lacking, and working to change them.

Don't be discouraged if your score is less than perfect. Communication is a skill that we all should be constantly working at improving. Stay alert for opportunities in which to practice effective communication, and keep these basic guidelines in mind:

- **Be clear.** Whether you're speaking or writing, try to avoid the opportunity for confusion or doubt. Say or write what you mean and keep it simple. Good communication isn't fancy—it's clear and understandable.

- **Stay in touch.** A workplace always has changes that need to be communicated to the people affected by them. Also, frequent communication is important for reinforcing expectations and keeping company goals and values at the forefront. Informed employees tend to be more invested in their companies and feel more connected.

- **Be up front and honest.** Employees sense when managers aren't being up front or are being evasive, and managers who lose credibility with their teams have a difficult time regaining respect. Don't offer misinformation or gloss over problems, but don't be an alarmist, either.

- **Don't leave anyone out.** In spite of good intentions, information that starts at the top often reaches a certain level and then stops, leaving some employees in the dark. This can create resentment and speculation regarding the information that wasn't received.

When Good Communication Is Especially Important

Good communication is always important, but in some instances, it's particularly crucial. New employees, employees who are tackling new situations or assignments, and employees who are experiencing performance gaps require special treatment in the communication department.

I know it's not always (or ever) easy to find time to sit down with an employee to make sure you've communicated expectations or other information effectively and that the employee fully understands that information, but it's worth it in the long haul. Undoing problems caused by poor communication takes a lot more time than getting it right in the first place.

PERFORMANCE GAP

Some managers downplay the importance of communicating expectations to employees. I don't know how many times a manager has said to me, "I don't need to do that. I know good work when I see it." My standard answer to that comment is, "But will your people know good work when they do it?" It's fine for you to understand the expectations you have of your employees. If your team members don't understand them, however, they'll perform what they consider to be good work, and you'll get what you get.

The amount of time you'll need to spend with an employee, whether a new hire, one experiencing changes, or one who has a record of mistakes, depends on the experience and level of the employee, how willing that employee is to make changes, and other factors. Some employees will understand your expectations much more easily than others, making your job easier. Your job as a manager, however, is to make sure every employee has a handle on job expectations and other matters and issues that affect their performances. Policies must be communicated and understood, the goals of the company must be made clear, and workplace culture should be communicated as well.

Effective communication isn't necessarily easy, but it's one of the most important qualities of a good manager, and one that's worth developing and practicing every day. Watch for employees who seem overwhelmed or confused, or who are making mistakes. Chances are, they just need clarification or another explanation of what is expected of them.

A New Employee

Ineffective communication between a new employee and a manager can get a working relationship off to a rocky start and result in problems down the road. Hiring a new employee can be a tedious and expensive undertaking, so it's important to start out right.

Regardless of the type of company or business you're with or what job a new employee has been hired to perform, good communication is critical on several levels. In addition to making sure new employees understand job performance expectations for the position, make sure they have a clear understanding of the company's mission and goals, know about the chain of command, and so forth.

New employees need to learn workplace basics, including key policies, safety issues, lunch hour, parking, and so forth. It may or may not be your job to handle those sorts of communications, but make sure that someone does so new hires don't feel lost or overwhelmed.

> **PERFORMANCE BOOST**
>
> New employees—those who have been on the job 90 days or less—account for a disproportionate percentage of employee turnover, and it's often due to the fact that they don't receive enough information to make them feel comfortable and know how to effectively perform their jobs. You can avoid this by communicating your performance expectations, preferably in writing, and getting ROC from the new hire.

Also make sure that the new employee meets her co-workers. Briefly explain the responsibilities of each person, and talk about how the team works most effectively together, the status of ongoing projects, and so forth. Once you've covered all the bases, remember to ask for ROC, while explaining to the new employee what ROC is and why it's valuable.

Without this sort of information, new employees can't understand how the company works or who does what, much less how they're expected to successfully perform their new job. Taking time up front to communicate important information and performance expectations will save a lot of time and headaches down the road.

Work Situation Has Changed

Managers sometimes overlook the importance of continuing communication with employees who have been around for a while, especially those who are meeting or exceeding expectations.

Often those employees can operate just fine without much supervision. However, workplaces are full of changes, and those changes need to be communicated to all employees, even those low-maintenance workers who seem to sail right along on their own.

Employees want to know what's going on around them, and if they don't know this, they'll try to figure it out on their own. This can result in speculation, rumors, and suspicion, none of which are productive to the workplace. If changes are coming or have already occurred, make sure employees know, and take time to communicate how those changes will affect them. Will they need to get more training? Will their work hours change? Times of change are stressful, and good communication is extremely important during those times.

Employee with a Record of Mistakes

Dealing with an employee whose performance is lacking can be stressful, and managers sometimes try to avoid it. As you already know, however, that's not a good idea. Effective communication with an underachieving employee is necessary for the team member to have a chance at boosting performance and regaining status as a productive employee.

It's your job to assess the situation and, working with the employee, try to figure out how and why mistakes keep occurring. Maybe there was ineffective communication in the first place and the employee never really understood what was expected. Maybe the employee isn't feeling well and can't afford to miss anymore work, or maybe something in his or her personal life is affecting performance. Or maybe the employee simply isn't a good fit for the job.

Whatever is going on, you need to communicate with the employee in a positive and effective manner to get to the bottom of the problem. Then you need to work together to figure out how to boost that employee's performance.

The Least You Need to Know

- Receipt of communication (ROC) is an effective but underused tool in ensuring that employees understand your expectations.
- Putting performance expectations into writing can benefit you and your employees.

- Good communication skills are one of the most important qualities of a manager.
- Effective communication is especially important with new or underperforming employees, or when changes occur.

Monitor and Assess Performance

Almost every employee has the ability to perform at a higher level. Average employees can become really good employees. Good employees can blast off to become great employees. And don't give up on your team members who aren't meeting expectations; most performance problems are fixable. In Part 2, you'll learn how to monitor how your team members are doing and give them the feedback they need to boost performance. We also address some common performance problems and discuss how you can get employees who need help back on track.

How Are They Doing?

In This Chapter

- How monitoring performance benefits you and your team
- Six methods of monitoring performance
- How to use what you learn to boost performance

Once you're confident that job performance standards and expectations are in place and your employees have a full and clear understanding of what, how, and why they're doing their jobs, you can sit back and relax.

That was a joke. You're a manager. You can never sit back and relax. Your next step is to learn how to monitor the performance of each employee to determine whether he or she is meeting, exceeding, or not meeting those standards and expectations that you worked so diligently to establish.

You can't boost an employee's performance without first knowing the level at which the employee is performing. In this chapter, you'll learn how to get a handle on how your team is doing, providing you with a launching pad for performance boosting.

Why Monitor Performance?

Assessing and noting how the members of your team are doing is important in determining whether they are on track for meeting their stated goals and objectives. Looking at the bigger picture, it helps you see the role your employees are playing in advancing the company toward its stated goals and objectives.

Every member of a team contributes, either positively or negatively, to the goals of the organization. An employee who exceeds expectations moves the organization ahead toward its goals, while an employee who underachieves holds it back. As a manager, it's your job to identify which employees are helping the company move forward and which ones may be holding it back.

Knowing how your employees are doing allows you to make adjustments when necessary to get them back on track. If you have an employee who hasn't been meeting performance expectations for three months, but you don't know that because you haven't been paying attention, you've missed three months worth of opportunities to help that employee get his or her performance back up to where it should be.

Keeping on top of employee performance is good for your employees because it keeps them on target to meet their goals. It's also good for you, because you're expected to be a productive manager. And it's good for the company, which continues to advance when its employees are meeting goals and expectations.

 PERFORMANCE GAP

Some managers avoid monitoring employee performance because they believe team members will be upset or think the manager is checking up on them. Believe me, passing on monitoring is not a good plan. Ultimately, it will negatively affect you and your employees. You don't have to be intrusive to keep up with how your employees are performing, but you do need to keep up.

Keeping track of how your employees are doing doesn't mean that you're going to be hovering over them all day, counting how many phone calls they make or checking your watch as they return from lunch. It means you're going to verify that the job performance expectations you've set are being met, to keep your employees and the company on track toward meeting their goals.

Let's look at six ways you can stay on top of how well your employees are doing, without coming off as an overbearing micromanager.

Six Proven Methods of Monitoring Performance

Monitoring employee performance isn't difficult, but you can't get it done by sitting at your desk. A concept called management by walking around (MBWA), introduced in 1982, is still considered good advice. Managers who aren't seen are not accessible, nor can they have a good handle on how their employees are performing. Managers need to interact with their team members to see what they're doing, hear their concerns and suggestions, and be able to help them improve in their jobs. MBWA entails spending at least 20 percent of your workweek out of the office and interacting with staff at every level. Managers are instructed to spend 80 percent of their MBWA time listening to employees and getting ideas for how they can work better.

PERFORMANCE BOOST

Learn more about MBWA from the book in which it was introduced, *In Search of Excellence,* by Tom Peters and Robert H. Waterman (see the Resources appendix).

The following six methods of monitoring, all of which involve inter-action with employees and/or customers, are tried and proven methods that will help you stay connected to your team and boost their performance levels.

Check In Regularly

Checking in with employees is probably the easiest means of moni-toring performance—and a very effective one. Checking in with your workers is as simple as the following examples:

- "Hey, Kyle, how's it going today? How's Martin's web-site coming along? You still on target for our meeting Thursday?"

- "Good morning, Shanna. You look busy today. What's your plan for getting those payment notices ready that need to go out with the four o'clock mail?"

- "How are you, Bob? I see you're in the middle of something here, but I need to talk to you about how we're going to display the holiday cookie collection. Why don't you stop by my office when you're finished and we'll see what we can come up with."

Check-ins should occur regularly and at about the same time so employees aren't caught off guard and get the idea that you're checking up instead of checking in. That doesn't mean you should approach team members only at scheduled check-in times, but do let employees know what to expect.

Checking in with team members makes you accessible and keeps you in touch with their day-to-day work and performance. Check-ins also eliminate the need for team members to seek you out, which could be distracting and an ineffective use of time. You'll learn to recognize when someone is having trouble meeting a deadline or when a project is running behind schedule. You'll also develop closer relationships with team members, most of whom will appreciate your interest. Regular check-ins are small investments of time and effort, with the potential for big results.

Have a Stand-Up Meeting

Also known as group huddles or morning roll calls, stand-up meetings are not meetings as we tend to think of them. They're short, to the point, and intended to keep everyone informed and up-to-date. There's no in-depth discussion, no long-term strategy planning— just a quick exchange of information, with clarification permitted as necessary.

If you're running a small shop or operation, you might want to include everyone. If you're a larger operation, limit stand-ups to key people, for the sake of manageability and expediency. Many companies find that daily meetings are the way to go, while others schedule them for just once or a couple times a week.

You should have a scheduled starting time for the meeting, but don't delay it if someone is not on time. Employees who are unable to attend the huddle should have colleagues deliver their reports, when possible. Stand-ups can be performed physically or virtually.

PERFORMANCE BOOST

The most successful stand-up meetings are limited to about 10 people. Any larger, and they tend to get bogged down and become unproductive. The point of a stand-up meeting is for members of the team to report what they've accomplished since the last meeting, what they plan to accomplish before the next meeting, and any problems they might be encountering that require help or direction from someone else.

Stand-up meetings generate organization and shared responsibility among team members. If Amanda tells the other six members of her team that she will finish sorting and hanging up the 24 boxes of jackets in the storeroom by the end of the day, she has set a goal for herself and committed in front of her peers to meeting that goal. Barring unforeseen problems or circumstances, she's very likely to meet that goal.

These meetings give you a chance not only to monitor who's meeting and exceeding performance goals and who may be encountering problems, but also witness the interactions of your team. You get to experience the cooperative attitude between Amanda and Jeanne, and pick up on some tension between Terrell and Jackie.

People stand at stand-ups for good reason: to keep them short and high energy. Stand-ups should be limited to no longer than 15 minutes, or even shorter for a small team.

Conduct a 360-Degree Assessment

A 360-degree assessment is the process of gathering information about an individual employee from a variety of sources, including superiors, peers, subordinates, and customers, when applicable. The information is processed and fed back to the individual, who compares it with his or her own self-assessment. A 360-degree assessment is more formal and time-consuming than a quick check-in or group huddle, but it can be a useful tool for establishing the performance level of team members.

Basically, a 360-degree assessment involves polling various people who have contact with a particular employee, to get an idea of how the employee is performing. The employee also is polled regarding his or her own performance, with those results then compared to the feedback collected from others. People involved respond to specific questions on a feedback form. You can either make up your own form or purchase a generic one developed for use within your business area.

The assessment process is valued because it necessitates a high level of involvement from different levels of associates, identifies problem areas and developmental needs, and calls attention to performance capabilities.

Some controversy exists regarding 360-degree assessments, as they require a good deal of time and can result in hurt feelings and defensiveness if they're not managed carefully. If you choose to use this method of monitoring employees, plan carefully before you start and make sure everyone understands the intent and purpose of the exercise.

Use Whiteboards

Whiteboards are excellent tools for keeping a handle on employee performance, especially when you're dealing with measurable goals and results.

Placed within sight of team members, a whiteboard can contain the number of phone calls necessary for each person to make within a specific time frame, the number of shipping crates that are to be unloaded that day, and so on. Workers who meet their goal can note their achievement on the board. Goals can be updated at planned intervals during the day, remaining in sight and clear to everyone involved.

Keeping goals in front of employees and tracking them as you go keeps workers accountable and ensures that everyone has the same expectations.

Use Formal Milestones and Measurements

Formal milestones and measurements are usually used to monitor progress during longer-term or more involved assignments and typically work well to keep employees on track.

Think back to Lee from Chapter 4, the manager of a team of information technology technicians. Lee's team was assigned to revise the online sales manual to make it more user-friendly for the sales force. It was a big assignment, and Lee would have done well to establish formal milestones and measurements to help his employees meet periodic goals so that they were sure to finish the project before the sales conference on March 1.

Let's say that team members learned of the assignment on December 22 and were instructed that the project needed to be completed by February 18, in advance of the March 1 conference. Lee would then set some intermediate goals, such as "The existing manual will be completely reviewed for content by January 8," "Sections that require revision will be identified by January 15," and "Flow diagrams that better illustrate procedures will be added to the manual by January 30."

CASE IN POINT

"Milestones and measurements" is just a fancy phrase for telling your employees how much you need by when. The milestone is the *when*, and the measurement is the *how much*. If you've got a project deadline of 50 percent completion by December 15, 50 percent is the measurement and December 15 is the milestone.

Setting milestones for those major goals provides everyone with the same expectations. Lee should follow up with check-ins and/or stand-up meetings to track progress of the project and give team members a chance to voice any concerns or problems. The milestones can be noted on a whiteboard and kept in front of the team to keep members motivated.

The term "formal milestones and measurements" may sound foreboding, but it's a sound means of monitoring performance and can make a project far more manageable and achievable than it might otherwise seem. Revising the online sales manual before the sales conference is a major assignment, but establishing milestones and measurements can keep the project moving ahead and eliminate a lot of anxiety.

Ask Your Customers What They Think

Customer feedback is a valuable tool in monitoring employee performance. After all, the customer is at the center of the performance management cycle and is the primary reason for the efforts of you and your team.

If your customers report that they're pleased with your product, or your sales associates have exceeded expectations, or your customer service representatives have been exceptionally helpful, you most likely are on track for meeting your goals in those areas. If, on the other hand, customers are noncommittal or dissatisfied, you know you've got to address the issue and figure out how to help your team members boost their job performance.

Collecting and putting customer feedback to use is increasingly recognized as essential to monitoring employee performance. Many major corporations, and a good number of not-so-major ones, have turned customer feedback into an art, employing sophisticated customer feedback management systems to track response at every level of their organizations.

Don't worry, though. You can still garner customer feedback the old-fashioned way: in person, with paper surveys, or over the phone, although many organizations (and customers) now prefer online questionnaires. Each of these methods has advantages and disadvantages; you'll learn more about gathering and using customer feedback in Chapter 14.

Response from your customers provides an accurate basis on which to gauge how well you and your employees are doing, and it should be used whenever it's feasible to do so.

Using What You Learn to Verify Expectations

Once you've observed your employees and gathered information, you can make some decisions regarding expectations. You'll see either that employees are meeting expectations and the expectations make sense, or that expectations need to be adjusted.

If all employees are finishing their daily work assignments by 2:15 and then standing around catching up on football scores and the results of the latest reality show until the shift ends at 3:00, you're going to have to adjust your expectations upward. If phone calls are not being returned because an employee is also responsible for processing all online merchandise orders, performance expectations may have to be adjusted to a lower level.

PERFORMANCE BOOST

Regardless of how you monitor employee performance, remember that it has to be done on a regular basis and that you can't base your opinion of performance on a one-time observation. You might observe an employee performing really, really well or doing something just awful, neither of which represent the typical performance of that particular worker. Monitoring performance should be practiced on a daily basis.

Verifying expectations should be done on both a short-term and long-term basis. Jake might be able to make only 12 of the 15 deliveries scheduled for Tuesday because of bad weather. That's understandable and requires a short-term adjustment of expectations. However, if he is consistently missing delivery deadlines, a longer-term assessment is necessary to determine whether the expectations are unrealistic or whether there's another reason for the performance gap.

Monitoring and assessing employee performance is a difficult task for managers who prefer to stay in their offices and assume that employees are meeting expectations. Smart managers, however, understand the importance of getting and keeping a handle on how their team members are doing, and realize that it establishes rapport, creates an atmosphere of camaraderie, and, in the long run, helps employees to excel.

The Least You Need to Know

- A good manager can stay on top of how employees are doing without being obtrusive or micromanaging.
- Tracking employee performance helps keep your team moving toward its goals and the goals of the company.
- Monitoring feedback can be a formal or informal process, but it's always interactive.
- Information gathered while monitoring performance is used to verify whether expectations are being met.

Giving Constructive Feedback

In This Chapter

- Why give feedback?
- Constructive feedback, both positive and negative
- How to deliver effective feedback
- The importance of regular feedback

Feedback comes in many forms and is applicable to nearly every area of our lives. If you think about it, we give and receive feedback all the time. It's how we get and process information. You get feedback—sometimes desired, sometimes not—at work, at home, when you're having lunch with a friend, or when attending a community event.

Feedback is absolutely essential when dealing with employees, and you won't successfully boost performance if you don't use it. When not used properly, however, feedback doesn't boost performance and can actually be counterproductive.

In this chapter, you'll learn why feedback is vital to healthy manager-employee relationships, when to use feedback, and how to use it effectively to benefit both you and your employees.

Everyone Wants and Needs Feedback

For our purposes, feedback is simply the process of providing information to an employee or group of employees regarding performance, to prompt them to maintain or improve performance. Feedback is at the heart of the coaching you need to engage in with your employees, and lack of feedback is a frequent complaint among workers. The U.S. Department of Labor tells us that the number one reason employees (voluntarily) leave their jobs is that they feel they're not appreciated. Sure, you'll run into employees who react defensively to feedback, even when it's intended only to be constructive and helpful. However, most employees want to hear how they're doing and improve their performance when possible.

One thing is certain: everyone likes to be recognized and praised for good work. If I spend a whole weekend trimming hedges, edging the lawn, and cultivating flower beds, I darn sure want my family and neighbors to notice and tell me how great the yard looks. The same goes for your employees. If Anthony goes above and beyond the call of duty and voluntarily stays after his shift ends to finish setting up the canned goods display at the front of the grocery store, it would be a serious mistake for his manager not to recognize that and provide him with feedback about his good work.

By the same token, if two customers in one week have complained about Jane's lack of attentiveness and reported that they had to wait at the checkout station for nearly 10 minutes before she was able to properly ring up and pack their items, Jane's manager needs to address the issues through feedback to Jane. If she doesn't, Jane's unacceptable behavior is likely to continue.

Basically, a manager has three feedback options:

- Offer positive feedback
- Offer negative feedback
- Offer no feedback

Let's take a closer look at those three options and the effect each tends to have on employees.

> **CASE IN POINT**
>
> Karen had worked in a supermarket bakery for several years. She was a dependable employee who could be counted on to perform her job well. Karen approached Maya, the bakery manager, and suggested they rearrange some items in order to showcase the more expensive, specialty desserts. Maya liked the idea and encouraged Karen to run with it. Within two weeks, sales of specialty desserts had increased substantially, and the store manager noticed. Maya let other employees and managers know that the move was Karen's idea. Karen was so empowered by the positive reinforcement that she assessed the rest of the bakery display and made other suggestions for improving it. Karen had a real knack for display and eventually ended up in charge of it storewide.

Positive Feedback

When you recognize good performance and provide positive feedback, you achieve several things:

- You show employees that you're attentive to their behavior.
- You demonstrate that you appreciate them and their efforts.
- You provide positive reinforcement.
- You motivate them to perform at even higher levels.

Rare is the employee who is completely self-motivated and constantly exceeds expectations solely to achieve personal satisfaction. Most employees won't perform at top level if they perceive that nobody cares or their performance doesn't matter. Feedback is a signal to your team members that you're observing their performances and that the manner in which they perform is important.

Providing feedback in the form of praise for good performance lets employees know that you acknowledge and appreciate their efforts, and that goes a long way. Some managers believe that praising employees is indulging them and that team members should be highly motivated to perform based on the fact that they're receiving a paycheck. However, those managers are missing a key opportunity to boost performance.

The Gallup Organization has polled more than four million employees around the world concerning managerial feedback, and the results are pretty conclusive. Sixty-nine percent of workers surveyed reported that praise and recognition from their bosses is more motivating than their salaries, and four out of five workers said that praise and recognition motivates them to perform at higher levels.

Letting employees know that you're pleased with their efforts positively enforces their behavior and affirms that they're performing at an acceptable or exceptional level. It sends a powerful message to keep on doing what they're doing, or to work to improve performance even more.

Members of your team will be motivated by positive reinforcement, but be careful not to overdo it. Constant praise for small efforts or achievements has the same effect on workers as it does on kids: they learn to expect it, it loses meaning, and they get cranky or anxious when they don't get it.

When Negative Feedback Is Necessary

Providing regular (not constant) positive feedback for good performance is appropriate and helpful, but it's unrealistic to think you won't sometimes need to offer negative feedback as well. When given properly, negative feedback can be as useful—perhaps even more so—than positive feedback.

Negative feedback should not be punishing or overly critical, and it should be presented in a helpful, nonjudgmental manner. This type of feedback simply points out a performance area or effort that requires improvement in order to make a team member aware that a change is needed.

PERFORMANCE GAP

When it's necessary to give negative feedback, make sure you don't come off as being apologetic or reluctant. Don't be arrogant, but try not to appear uncomfortable. Never say something like, "I'm sorry to have to tell you this …," or another phrase that could cause an employee to not take your feedback seriously.

Hardly anyone enjoys having to give negative feedback, but to not relate it is neither smart nor productive. Providing both positive and negative feedback establishes a sense of fairness and balance that's necessary for good morale and an environment that encourages employees to boost their performance levels. The trick is understanding how to give both types of feedback in a productive and constructive manner.

The Danger of Not Giving Feedback

Holding back from giving feedback is common among managers, especially when the feedback isn't positive. The effect of silence, however, can be harmful to your workplace and team members. Employees who get no feedback will shape their own beliefs about their job performances, and those beliefs might be quite different than your own. Someone who is meeting expectations but never gets any feedback might assume that everything is fine or, particularly if he or she is new and used to getting feedback, might become anxious and figure that performance is inadequate.

On the flip side, an employee can be experiencing all sorts of performance gaps and, if they're not addressed, continue right on, oblivious to those shortcomings. Even if the employee recognizes that performance is falling short, lack of feedback can serve as an excuse for him or her to not work toward improvement.

A lack of feedback conveys different things to different workers. Some will conclude that their work must be okay, others will think that their work isn't important, and a significant population will think that you simply don't care about their performance. You may be silent, but you're still saying something to your employees.

Avoiding feedback might be the easy way out, but you'll pay a price for that ease. Both positive and negative feedback is necessary if you're looking to improve performance and stay on track for your goals.

How to Give Good Feedback

Providing constructive feedback, both positive and negative, is a skill that managers need to practice in order to do well. Feedback can be offered in a manner that is either effective or ineffective. Ineffective feedback is not constructive and doesn't serve your goal of boosting performance. To be effective and constructive, feedback must …

- Be specific.

- Focus on behavior.

- Be timely.

- Be nonjudgmental and factual.

Consider a couple examples of effective and ineffective feedback, both positive and negative:

Ineffective: "Hey, Jake, that was a really nice presentation you gave this morning."

Effective: "Hey, Jake, the presentation you gave to the rest of your team this morning was really well organized and easy to follow, and the graphs you used were particularly helpful. I could see that everyone understood the information you presented, and I've noticed that several people have already implemented it in their work."

Ineffective: "Karen, you always forget to ask customers if there's anything else you can do for them."

Effective: "Karen, I've noticed twice this week that you've neglected to ask customers at the end of your transaction if there's any way you can be of further help. Is it just that you're forgetting to do that, or is there another reason?"

Notice that the effective feedback is specific, timely, nonjudgmental, and focused on behavior, whereas the ineffective feedback is vague. Let's look at those qualities a little more closely.

Be Specific

Let your team member know what you want to talk about, and be specific about what you've observed. It's okay to say, "Nice job today, Bob," but will Bob know that you're referring to the way he handled a call from a difficult client? If you've noticed that Sharon is reacting slowly when answering the phone and you advise her to "step it up a little bit the next time," will she understand that she needs to pick up the phone by the third ring?

If the feedback you offer isn't specific, it's likely to simply be taken as general praise or criticism, which isn't effective in reinforcing or changing behavior. Offer details about what aspects of an employee's performance that you like or about what behaviors need to be changed.

Instead of simply telling Bob that he did a good job, you could say something like this:

> I know that particular client can be difficult to deal with, Bob, and I really appreciate that you were able to maintain your cool. I also noticed that you asked all the right questions to get the information you needed, and that you were able to correct the problem and make sure the client was satisfied. That was a terrific effort on your part.

It's equally important to offer specifics when you need to provide negative feedback, such as in the case of Sharon. A better way to address her would be something like this:

> Sharon, I've noticed that the phone has been ringing more than three times before you get to it, and I'm wondering if there's a specific reason that you're having trouble answering it by the third ring. Let's work together to figure out a way to make sure it never rings more than three times before you pick up.

Offering this type of specific feedback might seem forced or contrived at first, but it will quickly become habit after you've practiced for a while. Just as you need to be clear regarding performance expectations, you need to provide specific feedback that can be understood and acted upon.

Be Timely

Praising someone for behavior that occurred two weeks earlier does little to reinforce that behavior or motivate the employee. And pointing out behavior that needs to improve well after the fact does not have the same impact as addressing it in a timely manner. In addition, the behavior is likely to have been repeated, resulting in further mistakes or problems.

An old adage states that praise should be immediate and negative feedback should be offered within 24 hours of the behavior that prompted it. That may not always be possible, but it's true that feedback given sooner is better than that given later. Perceptions and impressions tend to become distorted over time, increasing the chance that your feedback won't be as accurate if you wait to give it.

Be Nonjudgmental and Factual

Employee respect is seldom lost faster than by jumping to an inaccurate conclusion about a behavior or incident. Assuming that you know all the facts when you don't is dangerous because it forces you to rely on assumptions and your own judgments.

It's best not to offer feedback if you're not sure of what occurred or the circumstances under which the behavior occurred. If a behavior or incident requires your feedback because it's causing or has the potential to cause problems, be sure you gather as much information as possible before offering it. If more than one person is involved, be sure that everyone is heard.

Focus on Behavior

Feedback is about what an employee has done or hasn't done, not about the employee. A team member will quickly become defensive and alienated if she perceives feedback to be a personal attack. Avoid pointing the finger at an employee or sounding accusatory. Avoid using phrases that start with "you." Never say something like, "You always let the phone ring too long before you answer it." It's better to start a sentence with "I," such as "I've noticed that ...."

If Kevin has spent most of the last two team meetings texting underneath the table, don't tell him that he's rude and disinterested. Instead, point out to him that you're concerned that he's not engaging with the rest of the team and is missing important information that he'll need in order to remain on track to finish the project on time.

PERFORMANCE GAP

Some managers tend to offer feedback unadvisedly, without first considering circumstances. Never give an employee negative feedback in front of others, regardless of how urgent you feel the feedback is. If you're angry, take some time to cool off and think about how best to handle the situation. Acting impulsively could badly impact the respect level between you and your team.

Instead of praising Joanne as being a great communicator, tell her that her PowerPoint presentation was well organized and that you especially liked the use of bullet points to illustrate the information. Note that her commentary was succinct and matched the information presented on the screen.

Focusing feedback on an action or behavior will reduce the chance of a defensive or angry reaction from the employee. Most people can accept that they've made a mistake or could have done something better, but nobody likes to be made to feel inferior or stupid. Phrase your remarks in a manner that can't be interpreted as personal or overly critical.

Using Feedback as a Daily Tool

Some managers reserve feedback for formal performance reviews, but feedback should be a tool you reach for every day. In addition to performance reviews, feedback should be used when ...

- An employee meets performance expectations.
- An employee exceeds performance expectations.
- Performance gaps arise.

Many bosses are reluctant to offer feedback to employees, just as they're reluctant to specifically state their expectations for employee performance. This happens when managers buy into those employee myths you read about in Chapter 1—that team members know exactly what they're supposed to do and are capable of evaluating their own performance. Employees need to receive specific information about what they are to do, and specific and frequent information about how well they're performing. Feedback should not be reserved for performance reviews, but should be given every day, if applicable.

> **PERFORMANCE BOOST**
>
> A recent poll by the Gallup Organization revealed the following qualities about employees who receive regular praise and recognition at work: their individual productivity increases, they're less likely to quit, they interact more with their co-workers, they get higher performance ratings from customers, and they have better safety records.

Employees who meet expectations should definitely understand the level at which they're working. You don't want employees to interpret that they're working either above or below expectations, so it's necessary for you to offer feedback that acknowledges and affirms their efforts.

An overachieving employee wants and deserves positive reinforcement for his or her efforts and achievements, and will continue to be motivated by affirmations from you. Praise for exceptional effort breeds more exceptional effort.

Providing negative feedback to someone experiencing performance gaps can be unpleasant, but it is necessary and actually helps employees recognize areas in which improvement is necessary and come up with a plan for change.

Giving effective, constructive feedback is a skill to be employed not only in business settings, but in many areas of your life. Remember that the more you practice giving feedback, the easier and more natural it will become.

The Least You Need to Know

- Feedback is at the heart of coaching and is necessary to boost employee performance.
- Giving both positive and negative feedback is necessary.
- Giving no feedback will leave employees to draw their own conclusions.
- Feedback should be specific, timely, nonjudgmental, and focused on behavior.

Helping Average Employees Improve

In This Chapter

- Identifying average employees
- Why average employees need to step up their game
- Factors that keep average employees from advancing
- Rewards that motivate employees to boost performance

Average employees are good employees. They show up for work and do what's expected of them. They understand their roles and do their jobs. Managers like average employees because they tend to be easy to work with and don't require an abundance of attention. Average employees deserve a lot of credit, and they function very well.

However, average employees have the potential to become great employees—employees who exceed expectations and speed toward their goals. A manager who ignores that potential and doesn't work hard to boost the performance of an average employee is cheating both the employee and the company.

Every employee should be encouraged, coached, and mentored to do the very best work he or she is capable of. Managers can't perform magic and fill unmotivated workers with motivation, but they sure can use every trick they've got to get employees to understand that boosting performance is beneficial—to both the company and the employee.

In this chapter, you'll learn how to identify average employees and convince them to kick up their performance a notch or two. You'll learn that it's your job to raise the bar to motivate workers and to make them aware of the rewards that come with improved performance.

Identify Your Average Employees

You already know your average employees. Let's say they're Rafael in the receiving department, Sharon in the mailroom, and Jackson in customer service. They do what they're supposed to do and don't cause many problems. You're pretty happy with these employees.

If you ask Jackson to make sure he contacts the 12 customers whose shipments have been delayed, he'll make the calls. If you tell him the calls need to be made by noon, he'll get them done before he takes his lunch break. Sharon will get the mail delivered to every office by 11 A.M. and make sure that it gets back out by 4 P.M. Rafael will make sure that all the paperwork is in order when a shipment comes in and that the shipment gets to the right person within the company. These are good workers, but you know they could boost their performance to do even better.

Some qualities of an average employee include these:

- Dependable
- Willing to perform job tasks as requested
- Capable of performing most job tasks
- Often willing to take on new or additional tasks
- Often willing to learn in order to advance in the company
- Pleasant to work with and able to get along with peers
- Able to solve minor problems independently
- Able to work with and get along with customers, as necessary
- Somewhat interested in company goals and culture

Average employees have the capacity to achieve more than they do, and it's your job to teach them how and motivate them.

Why They Need to Improve Performance

Companies have undergone great changes during the past few years in response to an ailing national economy and other factors. Many companies have been forced to lay off employees or cut hours, wages, or benefits.

PERFORMANCE GAP

Avoid the tendency to overlook or even ignore average employees. You'll find that high-achieving and underachieving employees require more of your time and energy, but average workers who feel ignored will become demoralized and resentful, possibly enough so to make them slide right out of the average category.

As a result, in many workplaces, more work is expected from fewer people, and employees are expected to pick up the slack. While some employees view increased expectations as a welcome challenge, others are resistant to learning new skills and increasing productivity.

Average employees keep up with expectations but generally don't take the initiative to figure out a better method of performing a task or boost performance on their own. In today's workplace, however, with competition from both here and abroad, all employees at every level should be looking at how they might exceed expectations in order to establish value and ensure that their jobs remain secure in an insecure work environment.

Customers Expect More

Along with employers, customer expectations have been increasing as customers work hard to get the best products and services for their money. As the business world becomes increasingly globalized and competitive, the status quo doesn't work anymore. Customers demand better and cheaper products and services, delivered faster and more efficiently than ever.

That means employees need to constantly work harder in order to be able to continue meeting the increasing demands of customers. Some employees understand and react to this on their own, but others need your encouragement. You need to raise the expectations you set for them in order to boost their performances and keep your customers happy.

Because They Can

Just as you would encourage a bright, average-performing child to work harder in high school to ensure acceptance to college or a decent job after graduation, you need to encourage your average employee to do his best on the job.

Think of how frustrated you'd be (or remember how frustrated you've been) with a kid you knew could produce outstanding work but was content to coast along doing average work, thereby passing up entrance to a top-rate college.

If you have an employee who is meeting expectations when you know full well she can exceed them, you're not doing her any favors by allowing her to coast along instead of pushing her to excel. With effective leadership and increased levels of confidence and motivation, that employee could become a team leader who motivates others and helps to advance the entire operation.

Of course, you can't force an employee who's content to coast along to excel, and if her lack of ambition isn't holding the company back, it may be okay to simply accept her average performance. However, the employee should be made to understand how her attitude affects her position within the company, future salary increases, and so forth.

Don't ever put a lid on an employee's potential because it seems easier than coaching and motivating her toward the next level. That's bad for her, for you, and for the company.

Help Your Employees to Overcome Hurdles

So why aren't all employees high-achieving and motivated to perform? Most employees apply for a job because they both need and want it, right? We hear every day about the high unemployment rate and all the people who can't find jobs—it seems like those who are employed would be happy to be at work. Yet many employees never rise to their levels of competencies, and many managers never ask "why," or do more than assume that a lack of motivation is to blame.

The truth is, other reasons are behind employees remaining good workers instead of getting to be great ones. It's a tendency of workers, and people in general, to get comfortable with what they do and the way they do it. When that happens, inertia can set in. Others are afraid to push themselves because they fear they might fail. Still others simply don't like change and will actively go out of their way to avoid it. Let's look at these hurdles some employees face, and then you'll learn what to do about them.

Inertia and Complacency

When employees become comfortable in their jobs and don't meet with frequent challenges, they sometimes become complacent, even lackadaisical, regarding their work. Managers can unintentionally reinforce that behavior simply by allowing it to happen and can actually contribute to it if they allow complacency to set in.

Complacency occurs in all areas of life, not just the workplace, and has been blamed for events ranging from 9/11, to the demise of marriages, to the failings of businesses. It seems to be human nature to become complacent when things are going well, or at least moving along at status-quo level. If there's complacency at a company level, employees will mirror that attitude.

An average employee will often continue to do what's expected of him but, if not challenged and kept motivated, will not rise to the next level. A complacent manager tends to allow employees to move along at their own speed, foregoing the monitoring and feedback that's so important to boosting performance.

Complacency is dangerous to a workplace because it can cause the following to occur:

- Communication between management and employees decreases.

- Long-term goals become less important than daily tasks.

- Daily monitoring and feedback decreases.

- Problem solving does not happen on a proactive basis, but becomes reactionary.

- Decisions tend to be made quickly, without sufficient thought process.

- Employees blame one another for problems.

- Willingness to take leadership roles diminishes.

- There is reduced contact with customers and reduced effort in achieving customer satisfaction and loyalty.

All these factors, of course, are bad for both the company and your employees. As a manager, however, you can help your team avoid complacency by putting in place the steps discussed so far:

- Establishing clear job performance standards and expectations

- Communicating those expectations clearly

- Making sure team members understand the expectations

- Making sure they know how to do their jobs

- Monitoring and providing performance feedback

A manager wears many hats. You're a coach, a boss, a counselor, and a teacher. When it comes to preventing complacency and inertia, you're also a cheerleader. It's up to you to keep team members motivated and excited about their jobs, and invested in the long-term goals of the company.

Fear of Failure

Average employees sometimes remain at a certain performance level because they're afraid of failing at a higher level. I've seen employees turn down promotions for that reason—they're afraid they won't succeed at the next level.

If you suspect that one or more of your team members is avoiding rising to the next level for that reason, you'll need to pull out your best management skills, including coaching and mentoring, to increase confidence and boost performance.

PERFORMANCE GAP

Before you decide to target an employee for confidence boosting in order to help her move to the next level, be sure that she's capable of doing so. It's a mistake to encourage someone to progress to a job that she's not able to do. While it's your job to identify an employee who's reluctant to advance out of fear, make sure she's not holding back because she lacks the abilities to move on. Pushing someone who's not qualified to advance can result in frustration and demoralization.

Often an employee only has to try a new task or position and be given a little time to get acclimated before realizing that it's well within his or her level of ability—and a nice change from the day-to-day work as well.

Resistance to Change

Some employees are satisfied to remain where they are simply because they want to avoid any type of change. This is a different situation than employees who become complacent—that's more passive. Change resistance is active; some employees just do not like any type of change and will do everything in their power to fight it.

Most employees tend toward change resistance if they feel the change will threaten their status or job security. It's an employer's nightmare if all employees balk at an impending change; it can make implementing the change extremely difficult or even impossible. Some employees, however, challenge even small changes that could benefit them.

Employees resist change for some documented reasons:

- They don't understand what the change entails.
- They have misconceptions about how the change will affect them.
- They don't understand the purpose of the change.

Explaining change to your team members is much like outlining performance expectations. You need to explain some specifics:

- **What the change is.** "The company is switching to 4 10-hour work days instead of 5 8-hour days."
- **How it will affect the employee.** "Starting time will be 7 A.M. and we'll stay until 5:30 P.M., with a half-hour break for lunch. We will work Monday through Thursday."
- **Why the change is necessary.** "We've got to cut operating costs, and a survey the company commissioned showed that changing operating hours would be an effective means of doing so."

Be sure to give employees time to ask questions and express concerns. Your team members—like Sheila, described in the following scenario—will likely resist change much less if they have a full understanding of what the changes involve and why they're occurring.

Sheila's manager asked to see her one afternoon to talk about some changes that would be occurring within the customer service department. Sheila, who dislikes change of any kind in both her work and personal lives, was immediately on alert. Without knowing anything about it, she already had an idea that she wasn't going to like these changes. Anne, Sheila's manager, explained that Sheila would be taking on some of Karen's responsibilities in addition to her own. Anne explained which responsibilities would be added to Sheila's workload and told her she was confident that Sheila would be able to handle the extra tasks. She also told Sheila that she was scheduled for training the next week to prepare her for the added responsibilities and that her salary would be increased to compensate her for the extra work.

Predictably, Sheila was put off by the idea of change and told Anne as much. She didn't think she should have to take over Karen's work, Anne should have prevented this from happening to her, and she was sure she wouldn't be able to handle the extra work without starting work at 6 A.M. In fact, she was seriously thinking about quitting. Once Anne spent more time with Sheila and thoroughly explained the situation, however, Sheila understood the reason behind the change: the company had just landed a big new account that would require more customer service capacity. She calmed down when she realized her added responsibilities would not mean she'd have to start early or stay late, because she was going to have some help. And she actually started feeling a little excited to be a part of the company's advancement toward its goal of increasing its customer base.

Sheila at first made assumptions based on her resistance to change. Once Anne did a better job of explaining why the changes were occurring, how Sheila would be affected by them, and exactly what the changes would entail, however, Sheila bought into the changes and was ready to boost her performance.

Tell Employees How They'll Benefit

If you want your employees to boost their performance, you've got to raise your level of expectations and communicate those increased expectations to your team. Remember that we're considering your average workers, the ones who meet expectations.

If you raise the bar, chances are, they're going to raise their performance levels because they want to rise to the occasion and meet your expectations.

PERFORMANCE BOOST

Two of the most under-recognized rewards for employees are the simple act of recognition for a job well done and a sincere "thank you." If one of your team members exceeds expectations, be sure to utilize these two simple, yet extremely effective types of rewards.

On the other hand, employees will want something back from you. That's the WIIFH (what's in it for him) principle. You'll need to have a carrot to keep leading them forward and moving them toward their goals—and those of the company. You can motivate employees by informing them of how they might be rewarded for increased performance.

New Challenges

Employees who boost their performances above average and rise to new levels of expectations will look forward to new challenges as their job responsibilities increase. These employees may begin to demonstrate increased initiative as they gain confidence in their abilities and may actually seek out or request new challenges.

Let your average employees know that opportunities will be available for them when they begin to exhibit these characteristics. Assure them that their efforts will be recognized and appropriately rewarded with opportunities to develop new skills, learn more about the overall operation of the company, or perhaps even take on a new assignment with a new title.

Motivate them to exceed expectations by getting them excited about the challenges and opportunities in store for them. Of course, you need to be prepared to follow through with those promises in order to keep employees motivated and on board.

Increased Rewards

While some employees will be motivated by increased responsibility and challenge, others will need assurance of other types of rewards before they're convinced that boosting performance is the way to go. You'll read a lot more about using rewards to motivate employees in Chapters 17 and 18, but for now, remember that increased monetary compensation is not the only reward that's important to workers.

In addition to money and increased challenges and responsibility, your team members may be motivated simply by increased recognition, more flexible hours, opportunity for additional education or training, opportunity for greater input, and so forth. Your job is to identify what sorts of rewards are motivating to each employee and use those rewards to convince average employees to boost their job performances.

The Least You Need to Know

- Average employees are sometimes overlooked because they already meet expectations.
- Average employees might want to boost performance but have something preventing them from doing so.
- Your job as a manager is to motivate average employees to become better than average.
- Employees will want something in return for boosting their performance.

Motivate Top Performers

High-potential employees are important assets to any company, and managers should be deliberate about cultivating relationships and working with them to help these employees achieve and advance.

It's a mistake to think that because these exceptional employees are self-motivated, they'll boost their own performance without any help from you. High-potential employees thrive on challenge and involvement. Those who feel that they're not valued and important to the organization will look for challenges elsewhere.

Your job is to identify the high-performing members of your team and use the tools available to you to keep them motivated, excited, and advancing toward their goals.

Identifying Your Best Employees

A high-potential employee is generally defined as one who has the abilities, desire, and drive to advance to higher positions within an organization. These employees possess qualities that can inspire their peers to perform at higher levels, as well as the motivation necessary to work toward their own goals. Some qualities of employees who exceed expectations include these:

- Consistently perform better than what is expected
- Anxious to advance within the company
- Become bored with usual job tasks
- Eager to take on new or additional tasks
- Seeks direction in order to be able to move ahead
- Displays leadership qualities among peers
- Works as a self-starter
- Actively seeks solutions to problems
- Thinks outside of the box and is creative
- Is invested in company goals and culture
- Desires to be an active part of the team and the company
- Is persistent and doesn't give up
- Has a positive, "can do" attitude

Many of these high-achieving employees stand out as obvious leaders. You'll notice them helping or advising co-workers, and they'll talk to you about their role within the company or offer suggestions for a better way of performing a task.

Other top performers are not as easy to recognize. They might be a bit shy and not as likely to move to the forefront of the workplace. They might have great ideas but are reluctant to share them during meetings or even during their performance reviews. They work quietly, without the fanfare some employees exhibit. It's important that you recognize these workers, because they're just as valuable to your team as the more obvious leaders.

PERFORMANCE BOOST

Nonobvious top performers—those who aren't eager to share their ideas or initiate a conversation about their futures—tend to get passed over when it comes time for promotions or advancements. Be sure to encourage these members of your team to participate and remain engaged in the workplace, in order to attract the attention necessary for advancement.

You will discover these quiet but high-achieving employees as you observe them on a daily basis. As you identify them, you also must begin to coach and mentor them toward boosting their performances to even higher levels. A simple but effective means of determining your top-level employees is to ask yourself, "Which workers could I not do without?"

Your high achievers are integral to your team and set the tone for the rest of your workers. Other workers will follow the leads of these employees. If your top team members are excited, encouraged, and motivated, chances are good that other employees will be as well. If they're discouraged and unmotivated, however, your entire team will suffer.

Getting High Performers Excited About Their Futures

Once you know who they are, you can start working on getting—and keeping—your high performers excited about their futures. You want those futures, of course, to be within your company and to benefit both you and the other employees. To ensure those things, you've got to give them reasons to stick around and continue working at and above their current performances.

Make sure you're prepared before you meet with a top performer to discuss future plans and goals. These workers likely expect more of you than lesser-achieving team members, so be sure that you anticipate questions and concerns, and make sure you have a clear view of where the employee might be heading within the company. You can't talk productively with someone about his or her future if you don't have a good idea of what it might entail.

PERFORMANCE GAP

When discussing a top employee's future within your organization, be very careful that you don't make promises you can't keep or aren't qualified to offer. For instance, don't assure an employee that he or she will be part of management in two years unless you have ultimate authority over that decision. Say instead, "In my opinion, you are management material. I can see you as a manager in two years." Making impossible promises is a sure means of turning top employees into other-job-seeking employees.

Employees who exceed expectations need to be continually challenged. Don't get complacent with them, and never say something like, "Just keep doing what you're doing." These workers don't want to keep doing what they're doing—they want to move on to the next level and do something that will bring new challenges, recognition, and rewards. They're committed to continued improvement, and it's your job to help them identify opportunities for doing that.

What's in Your Toolbox?

High achievers are motivated by the same things average workers are, but they're also motivated by other factors that might not be so appealing to employees who are content just to meet expectations and call it a day.

Workplace fairness, sufficient compensation, clear appreciation, effective communication at work—those are factors almost everyone desires. Employees who consistently exceed expectations, however, also are attracted to opportunities and situations such as advanced training or the opportunity to be involved in decision making, the very things not-so-motivated employees stay away from whenever possible.

Keep in mind that some employees view as a reward the situations others view as punishment. For example, a highly motivated, high-achieving employee will likely welcome an opportunity to get involved in decision making or acquire additional responsibility. A different sort of employee, on the other hand, might rebel at the thought of being assigned additional tasks.

That's why it's important to know your employees, understand their performance abilities and levels, and figure out what they consider rewards versus drudgery.

Special Assignments and Projects

Special assignments and projects are an effective means of rewarding motivated employees, and they also keep high-achieving employees excited and eager to do their best.

When motivating a high-potential employee with a special assignment or project, explain why you think the project is right for him or her. Point out the attributes the employee possesses that make you confident in his or her ability to complete the project successfully. Take time to discuss how your team member will approach the project, and, just as with any assignment or task, be sure to communicate your expectations and make certain the employee understands them by confirming receipt of communication (see Chapter 4).

Be careful not to impose an assignment or project on employees who may have a good reason for not wanting it. While trying to keep workers excited and motivated, you could actually end up demoralizing them, as happened with Linda, described in the following scenario. (This rule, of course, pertains to all of your employees, but because your motivated employees are willing to undertake more extra work than others, it's particularly applicable to them.)

Linda was an exemplary office staff member with an investment advisory firm. She excelled at nearly every task, was interested in learning more about business, and often remarked that she would like to go back to school and earn a degree that would qualify her to work as a financial advisor. Thinking that he was doing something that would further motivate this high-achieving employee and get her excited enough to begin classes, Linda's boss asked her to take on the assignment of exploring some investment options for a client.

What he didn't know was that Linda's father had recently suffered a stroke, and she was very involved in his caretaking. Linda would have been thrilled with such an assignment during normal times, but she already was overwhelmed with work, her kids, her dad's care, up-keep in her house, and so forth. Although the assignment was well meant, it turned out to be a big imposition that caused Linda a great deal of anxiety and stress. Fortunately, she felt comfortable enough with her boss to explain her circumstances, and he immediately rescinded the assignment and offered to allow her to adjust her work hours, as necessary.

PERFORMANCE BOOST

Hopefully, you know your employees well enough to have a feel for what types of assignments or projects will be welcomed and motivating, and which might be intrusive and unwanted. If you're not sure, ask before making the assignments.

Advanced Training Opportunities

The same employees who get excited about additional assignments and projects will welcome advanced training opportunities because they look at them as chances to increase their value and job potential.

If your high-achieving employees would value advanced training or educational opportunities, try to make it possible for them to participate. Help with costs, if applicable, or give them some time off to make the training or educational experience more doable. Help them identify the type of training or courses that would be most useful and determine how they might best proceed.

Again, it's important to set and effectively communicate your expectations. If Rhonda and Jake will be spending two hours every afternoon for two weeks in a software development class, be sure they understand what you expect for them to accomplish and how their new knowledge and skills will be employed when they return.

PERFORMANCE GAP

Be careful to avoid the appearance that high-achieving employees receive preferential treatment, or that average or underachieving employees are denied opportunities. Policies such as tuition reimbursement must apply to everyone. Company-wide policies and specialized training for highly motivated employees, however, are two different things, and employees should be informed of that.

Greater Responsibility and Autonomy

Again, whereas some employees try to avoid taking on more responsibility, high achievers often thrive on it. Increased responsibility makes them feel that they're making bigger contributions to the success of the company and that their roles are more important. They use increased responsibility as tools for getting promoted or moved to a different position within the company.

Greater autonomy is also appealing to self-starters who feel confident enough to tackle jobs on their own and finish them successfully.

> **PERFORMANCE GAP**
>
> While attempting to motivate high-achieving employees with increased autonomy, make sure you don't shut them out of the loop and end up making them feel alienated and forgotten. There's a tendency to not provide a lot of feedback to your best employees because they do so well on their own, but that's a dangerous practice.

You can increase a high-achieving employee's responsibilities and autonomy by having him or her train a new employee or serve as a mentor to one who is experiencing difficulties with a particular aspect of the job. You can add to responsibilities an employee already has, such as making him or her responsible for displaying all the bakery items as well as overseeing their production, or by removing the need to check with you before making certain decisions. All these actions will keep a high-potential employee excited about the job and what the future could bring.

Involvement in Decision Making

Inviting high-potential employees to get involved in decision making is an excellent way to keep them happy and eager to take their performances to even higher levels. Being involved in decision making boosts morale and increases self-confidence levels, and it further invests employees in both their jobs and the mission of the company.

If Linda, the office staff member at the investment advisory firm you read about earlier, is asked to be involved in deciding whether the company should relocate its office, for instance, she'll be invested in either relocating or keeping the office where it is. Even if she disagrees with the ultimate decision, she'll understand the process of how it was made and the reasoning that contributed to the decision. Having that knowledge is not only empowering for Linda, but it allows her to share it with other staff members who weren't involved in the process.

Motivated employees especially should be involved in decisions that affect them and their co-workers. Always involve some employees, when possible, in decisions such as whether to change working hours, whether to shorten the lunch break, or where to hold the holiday party. Not doing so can negatively affect employee morale and is not conducive to boosting performance.

Exposure to All Aspects of the Business

Bob is a high-performing employee, but if he's confined to the same office to perform the same job for an extended period, chances are good that you'll watch as his motivation and performance level plummet. If you take Bob out of his office, however, and assign him to the shipping and receiving department so that he learns how that works, and then move him to the procurement side of the business for a while, and then have him work with the operations manager for three months, chances are good that he'll be happy and motivated as he learns how pieces of the business fit together to help the operation run smoothly.

Remember that most high-performing employees are looking to increase their value to the company because they're hoping to move forward and get ahead. If you've identified Bob as a valuable asset to the company and want to retain him as an employee, giving him an overall view of how the business runs can be highly beneficial.

Moving an employee from position to position isn't always practical, of course, and it doesn't work if no other employee can pick up the work Bob leaves behind when he moves from shipping and receiving to procurement, or if nobody is available to train and mentor him in his new position.

If you can make it happen, however, providing a top employee with a look at the whole business can pay off. If you really believe the employee is a winner, you might talk about succession planning and what opportunities may lie ahead.

PERFORMANCE GAP

While it's fine to share your visions for a bright future with a highly motivated, promising employee, be careful not to make any promises you may not be able to keep. Telling an employee that he'll be in a managerial position within six months when there isn't a position available is irresponsible and can jeopardize your credibility and relationship with a talented worker.

Getting the Most from Your High-Potential Employees

High-performing employees are desirable and necessary to your team, but they can present some challenges as well. They tend to require more of your attention than average employees because they'll push you for greater challenges, seek opportunities for development, offer suggestions you'll have to deal with, and so forth.

Frankly, high-potential employees are sometimes high-maintenance employees as well. Most of them aren't afraid to tell you what they think, even if their opinions are not in sync with yours. Some will not only offer suggestions regarding how they can do their jobs better, but may have suggestions concerning your job as well.

Your temptation might be to keep these employees busy and hope that they proceed pretty much on autopilot, leaving you to worry about improving the performance levels of the rest of your team. If you do that, however, you're depriving yourself of close contact with your most interesting and engaged employees, and you risk having them become demoralized and de-energized.

It's important that you make time to observe and coach high-performing employees. You might consider having several of them work on a project that you oversee but doesn't require a great deal of hands-on attention. That keeps high achievers busy and engaged, while giving you time to work with other members of your team.

During good economic times, top achievers can be rewarded with additional money as they move through the ranks. If you're not in a position at the present time to pay more, you'll need to employ some of the tools discussed earlier in the chapter. Try them out and see which ones your high-potential employees respond to most favorably. If increased training seems to be the best motivator, by all means, offer additional opportunities.

Regardless of what tools are available to you, the most effective ones are your attitude and willingness to work with these valuable employees. Mentor them, coach them, encourage them, and do whatever else you need to in order to keep them committed, involved, and on board.

Remember that the most-cited reason an employee remains in or leaves a job is either satisfaction or dissatisfaction with a boss. High-potential employees can keep you busy as you work continuously to keep them challenged and motivated, but they are human assets that require care and nurturing if they are to continue to grow.

The Least You Need to Know

- High-potential employees share characteristics that set them apart from others.
- High-potential employees need to be continually challenged in order to remain motivated.
- Your job as a manager is to identify means of motivating top performers.
- High-potential employees can be challenging, but it's well worth your time and effort to keep them happy.

Fix Problem Performance

In This Chapter

- Recognizing and addressing problem performance
- Knowing when to let it go
- Dealing with common problems
- Realizing the importance of following through

In a perfect company in a perfect world, every employee would meet or exceed expectations. In a real company in the real world, though, some employees fall behind and don't meet expectations. When that happens, it's your job to find out what's causing the substandard performance and to work with the employee to figure out a plan to raise the performance level to an acceptable standard.

It's easy to get impatient with employees who aren't meeting expectations, but if you believe that a member of your team has the ability to improve and become more productive, you can take steps to help him or her achieve that.

Helping employees solve performance gaps should be exactly that— an exercise in problem solving, not a punishment. Every employee will make mistakes somewhere along the way. Your job as a coach and manager is to try to ensure that performance gaps are as few and far between as possible, and to address and fix them when they do occur.

Recognizing and Dealing with Performance Problems

If you've established job expectations and standards, communicated them effectively, consistently monitored employee performance, and remained attentive to what goes on in your workplace, performance problems should be easy for you to identify.

For example, you'll know if Jack isn't getting outgoing mail collected in time to meet the pickup schedule. Another employee will mention the mail problem, or you'll see packages with incorrect shipping addresses returned as undeliverable. Likewise, you'll know if Alexa hasn't been following up with guests to make sure they were happy with their experiences at your day spa; you'll notice on her e-mail log that she didn't contact some guests.

You'll also know if Ray didn't get to the customer's house to clear the clogged drain by 2 P.M. as promised, because the inconvenienced customer will call to complain about it.

When you recognize a performance problem, it's your job to address it with the employee and to help your team member come up with a solution for fixing the problem.

PERFORMANCE GAP

In that perfect company in the perfect world, an employee would recognize a performance problem before you did and take steps on his own to fix it. In real-world companies, however, employees sometimes are not even aware of performance gaps or are unwilling or unable to take action to correct them.

Most of us don't enjoy having to confront poor performance, but it's necessary for both the other members of your team and the employee who's underperforming. Employees who don't recognize a problem can't correct the problem, so you've got to bring it to their attention.

Allowing a performance problem to go unchecked can bring down the performance of an entire department or even a company. And other employees who are aware of the problem will be looking to you to do something about it. If you don't, they'll be certain to speculate about your lack of action. So resist the temptation to put off confronting poor performance, and deal with it promptly.

Figure Out What's Causing the Gap

The first thing you want to do is figure out what's causing the performance gap, and the best way to do that is to ask the employee who's not meeting expectations what's going on. Listen to the employee talk about the problem. Hearing his or her thoughts on why it's occurring will help you understand the situation and give you clues to the direction in which you need to proceed.

Generally, employees don't meet expectations for six reasons:

- **They don't know what's expected.** You understand by now how important it is to clearly define expectations and make sure employees understand them. For example, Carl may be underperforming because he simply doesn't understand that a spreadsheet is a requirement of the report he's working on.

- **They don't know how to do what's expected.** Ryan may know perfectly well that his job is to clean the grocery store's walk-in cooler, and he may be willing to do it, but because nobody told him what that entails, he may not know how to do it.

- **They can't do it.** Sometimes extenuating circumstances prevent an employee from performing up to expectations. Maybe the electricity goes out or the computers go down. Maybe Randy doesn't have the physical strength to load the crates onto the truck and he's too macho to ask for help. Maybe Cindy fails to ask shoppers to sign up for a club card because she's incredibly shy and it's way beyond her comfort level to approach strangers. An employee might even have something going on in her personal life that's so distracting or disturbing that she's unable to concentrate well enough to complete her work.

- **They don't understand job priorities.** Rebecca may know she's got to have the grant proposal finished by noon, but she's not making much progress because she's obsessing over finding exactly the right words and making sure her punctuation and grammar are perfect. She's missing the big picture of finishing the proposal and getting it to her boss to review (and fix the punctuation and grammar, if necessary) and getting too caught up in worrying about details of the job.

- **They consider something other than the job to be more important.** Jack may know that the mail has to be collected in time to meet the pickup schedule, and he really has good intentions of getting it done. For some reason, though, he thinks it's more important to review his interoffice e-mail every day before he gathers the mail, and that task sometimes takes longer than he anticipates. On those days, the mail doesn't get collected in time for pickup, and Jack's coworkers aren't happy.

- **They don't want to do it.** This is a difficult situation to deal with because it often involves attitude problems and raises issues of discipline. Unfortunately, however, most managers will run into the scenario at some point when an employee doesn't perform a particular task or do a job just because he doesn't feel like it. Ryan may be okay with every aspect of cleaning the cooler except mopping up the floor. The mop bucket is heavy and unwieldy to drag around, and it gets really cold in the cooler when you're working with water. He doesn't like to mop the floor, so he doesn't do it.

As you talk with your underperforming employees, keep in mind these six reasons for poor performance. It's a good bet that they'll fall into one of them.

Addressing the Problem

Addressing the issue of poor performance with an employee is a three-step process. I've come up with the FEW method to help you remember the steps:

- State the *facts* concerning the performance gap.

- Share the *effect* the gap has caused.

- Ask *why* the problem occurred.

If you approached Rebecca about the problem with the grant proposal, for instance, you'd start out by giving her the facts, and telling her what you know:

> Rebecca, you didn't get the grant proposal finished in time for me to review it and get it submitted before the deadline.

PERFORMANCE BOOST

Don't be caught unprepared if an employee becomes emotional or is resistant to your observations regarding his performance. Some employees will become defensive or perceive that you're attacking them. It's your job to remain calm and stick to the facts regarding the situation.

In the next step, you share the consequences or effect of her failure to finish the work on time:

> We won't be considered for that grant since we missed the deadline. That means we'll have to try to identify another grant possibility and start working on another proposal. That will increase our costs and cause some difficulties with our budget.

Once you've stated the facts and effect, turn the discussion over to Rebecca by asking her to explain why she didn't get the proposal done on time. Once you've asked the question, just listen, but listen carefully.

In Rebecca's case, she didn't get the proposal finished on time because she couldn't prioritize the importance of different parts of the task. It could have been, however, that she couldn't finish it because the office computers weren't working or she lacked information she needed and was unable to contact the person who could supply it. She might have just found out her husband has a serious illness and is too upset to concentrate on her work, or she didn't understand the process of writing a grant application. She could have just been completely overwhelmed by the process of writing a grant application and didn't want to admit she didn't know how to do it.

Once you understand why the gap occurred, restate your expectation for the job and ask the employee for ideas on how he or she can prevent the problem from reoccurring. As tempting as it will be to throw out a bunch of solutions, use this opportunity as a coaching moment and give the employee time to think through the situation and come up with a plan for fixing the problem. The employee needs to own both the problem and the solution.

PERFORMANCE BOOST

Seek feedback from a trusted colleague on how you've dealt with an underperforming employee. Explain how you handled the situation and then ask your colleague for his or her thoughts. Were you understanding and willing to give the employee a chance to explain, or might you have come across as being abrasive, intimidating, or judgmental?

Once the employee comes up with a plan, take time to go over it together. Make sure you both understand what the problem entails, why it happened, and how it's going to be corrected. Make sure you make and keep coaching notes throughout this process, and be sure to follow up with the employee regarding his or her progress.

The last step in addressing a performance problem is to follow through and recognize the employee's efforts once the problem has been fixed. In a conversation with the employee, convey what you've observed regarding his or her performance. If performance has improved, be sure to offer encouragement and praise. If it has not, ask how you can be of further help and what the employee feels is holding back improved performance. Ask for employee input and pay attention to any concerns he or she may have.

Decide Whether the Problem Is Worth Fixing

Although performance gaps should never be ignored, be aware that sometimes they're not worth the effort of fixing. If the gap is minimal, it might make more sense to adjust expectations to accommodate the performance than to insist that the performance change to meet expectations.

For example, if the expectation is that the mail gets delivered by 1 P.M., but the employee responsible for the mail can't get it out until 2 P.M. because of other responsibilities, and a later delivery isn't holding anyone else back from completing their work, don't worry about it. Change the expectation to mail delivery by 2 P.M. and hold the employee accountable to that.

If it's a huge gap that you've addressed numerous times, with no improvement seen, it might be time to consider reassigning the employee or letting him or him go.

PERFORMANCE GAP

If you decide that a performance problem isn't significant enough to try to change, don't be tempted to ignore the issue with the employee. You should still let the employee know that you've recognized the gap but that you've decided the consequences aren't significant enough to address. If you don't acknowledge the problem, the employee might infer that performance gaps, regardless of their magnitude, don't matter.

Some performance problems, however, definitely need to be both addressed and corrected:

- **The gap affects other areas of the business.** Most businesses are interconnected. If something not getting done in your department affects the operation of another department, the problem needs to be fixed.

- **The performance problem keeps others from meeting their goals.** If Jack's failure to get the mail out on time means that Charley's job proposal won't get to a prospective client on time, Jack's performance gap needs to be resolved.

- **The gap will get bigger if not resolved now.** Little problems can become big problems. You need to judge whether a small performance gap has the potential to become a big one; if so, address it now.

- **Not fixing the problem sends a message that the goal isn't important.** If the goal of the department is to have every team member reach 10 potential customers every day, but Gary is reaching only 7 or 8, what does that say to the rest of the team about their performances and the goal for the department if you ignore Gary's gap?

- **The gap might indicate a bigger performance problem.** If Gary isn't reaching 10 potential customers a day, as expected, it might be a good idea to check up on what else he is doing—or not doing.

Deciding whether a performance problem is worth the time and effort to fix requires judgment on your part. If you let it go, however, remember to keep an eye on the situation. If gaps continue to occur, you definitely need to look at the bigger picture and address the matter with the employee.

Common Problems and What to Do About Them

Certain performance problems are common, meaning that most managers have to deal with them at some point in their work lives. Let's look a little more closely at some common problems, such as absenteeism and inability to get along with other employees. But remember that nearly every performance gap should be dealt with using these steps:

1. Identify the problem.

2. Figure out why the problem is occurring.

3. Address the problem.

4. Have the employee take ownership by coming up with a solution to the problem.

5. Follow through by recognizing efforts for improvement.

6. Keep careful coaching notes throughout the process.

Let's look more specifically at some of the problems you're likely to encounter.

High Absenteeism

A job can't get done if a team member isn't there to do it. The problem with absenteeism is that it often impacts other members of the team. For example, if the brochure copy doesn't get written because Aaron is absent again, that means Kate can't move ahead with the design, the printing has to be put on hold, and Lee has to explain to the client that the brochure won't be ready by the end of the week, as promised.

Chronic absenteeism is a performance gap that you need to address. Sure, everybody gets sick, and if your employee has a chronic health issue, that could be a valid reason for increased absenteeism.

PERFORMANCE GAP

If you start experiencing high absenteeism rates across your department, you need to take a hard look at yourself and your management style to determine whether the absenteeism is meant to be sending you a message.

Often, however, employees call in for reasons other than actual sickness, and that's what needs to be addressed. When seeking the cause for high absenteeism rates, ask yourself some questions:

- Does the employee seem content at work?

- Could something going on in the employee's personal life be contributing to increased absenteeism?

- Is something at work upsetting the employee or making his or her work experience unpleasant?

- Does the employee feel that his or her efforts at work are appreciated?

- Could the employee be looking and interviewing for another position?

- Does the employee have a drug or alcohol problem?

Once you get to the bottom of why the absenteeism is occurring, you and the employee can come up with a plan for solving the problem.

On-the-Job Absenteeism

On-the-job absenteeism, which basically means an employee is physically present at work but not performing the job he or she is expected to, is on the rise, probably because of the increasing number of potential distractions.

Many employees not only check their work e-mail, but also read personal mail, Twitter, MySpace, Facebook, and maybe a blog or two. They might be listening to music, texting with friends, gambling, checking on stocks, reserving vacation space, paying bills, shopping, or playing games—all activities that are easily accessible on any computer that hasn't had websites blocked with special software, or through employee's cell phones, PDAs, or laptops.

Studies have indicated that American businesses lose billions of dollars a year in productivity due to non-work-related Internet use. Some companies are taking advantage of social networking sites and blogs and are using them as ways to reach customers or as marketing tools, but many managers are unaware of how much time employees might be spending on activities that are in no way work related. In fact, Internet addiction has even been recognized as an actual condition, in which people are unable to avoid using the Internet.

If you suspect that one or more of your employees is spending excessive time online, consider solving the problem by installing blocking software or tracking software that will let you see the websites employees have visited. Be aware, however, that employees could still be accessing the Internet on their personal cell phones or PDAs. If your organization doesn't already have a formal Internet use policy in place, think seriously about establishing one.

Internet use is probably the most common reason for on-the-job absenteeism these days, but old-fashioned reasons such as excessive chatting, gossiping, and flirting are still factors.

Poor Safety Record

Safety violations or a poor safety record are serious performance gaps that need to be addressed. No workplace can afford to take chances with employee safety.

Problems concerning safety can be linked to an individual or individuals, or could be an organizational issue that needs to be addressed on a companywide scale. Strong debate in some industries centers on whether employees should share responsibility in workplace safety, or whether it is the sole responsibility of the employer.

If your company doesn't have a formal safety policy in place, establish one as soon as possible. Not having a policy raises all kinds of liability issues in the event of an accident. Even if your business is not one in which injuries are likely to occur, consider the fact that an employee could fall down the steps or slip on ice. Once a policy is in place, it's your job to make sure employees know about it, understand it, and follow the regulations it sets.

Any employee who doesn't perform according to safety standards should be considered a poor-performing employee, and the problem should be addressed appropriately.

Inconsistent Work Pattern

An inconsistent work pattern can be especially frustrating to a manager because you don't know what you can expect from the employee displaying it. Can you count on Trisha to finish the report, or not? Will Chuck get the load delivered on time, or not?

Lack of consistency can affect other members of the team, relationships with customers, and the performance level of the entire organization. This is definitely a performance problem that needs to be addressed, and one in which a solution can generally be identified.

This performance gap can stem from a wide variety of causes, meaning you'll need to address it carefully, after spending ample time working to determine possible causes. You might find that the employee doesn't realize performance is inconsistent or is having problems with a certain area of work. See if you notice a pattern in when the inconsistencies occur. If Trisha always finishes other reports on time but has experienced gaps when working on reports dealing with municipal water regulations, she might not have a good understanding of the intent or implementation of the regulations, making it difficult for her to complete her work.

Pattern of Mistakes

As with inconsistent behavior, a pattern of mistakes is a performance problem that occurs for a variety of reasons. You need to assess the situation carefully and ask yourself some questions:

- Do the mistakes occur at any particular time?
- Is the employee dealing with a particular topic when mistakes occur?
- Does the employee realize he or she is making the mistakes?
- Was anything different going on in the workplace when the mistakes occurred?

The best way to handle this performance gap is to address it with the employee and work together to come up with a solution. It's important for your team member to be involved.

Missed Deadlines

Missed deadlines are another highly correctable performance problem when you get the employee accountable for coming up with a plan to get the work done on time.

Have the team member explain to you the circumstances under which the deadline or deadlines were missed, and then ask for ideas on how to avoid the problem in the future. If Clayton tells you he missed the deadline because he got the dates mixed up, you can try to guide the discussion toward using online calendars or prompts as reminders, having him write himself reminder notes, or making sure he checks in with you at regular intervals to tell you what's going on and what's coming up.

If missed deadlines are caused by an inability to prioritize work, you'll need to counsel your employee on how to determine which jobs are most important and how to establish an order of work. Be prepared to spend some time on that task, as trouble prioritizing can cause problems for your employee and the rest of your team.

PERFORMANCE BOOST

If an employee missed a deadline because there was too much work to finish in too short a time, you may have to adjust unreasonable expectations.

Can't Get Along with Others

An employee who can't get along can be a big problem for a manager and the rest of the team. A single disgruntled employee can cause turmoil within a workplace, and a disgruntled workplace is not a happy or productive one. It's nearly impossible to boost the performance of employees who are sitting around fuming over what someone else said, or an advantage that didn't come their way, or a minor change in the time of their lunch break.

An employee who can't get along with others and is causing problems should be dealt with quickly and decisively, and the best way to do that is to meet and talk about the situation. Be open-minded; reasons you don't know about could be making the employee grumpy and difficult. Do, however, make it clear that the employee needs to come up with a plan for changing this attitude if he or she wants to remain a part of the team.

Disagreements can result when employees have different styles of communicating, or between different generations of workers with varying expectations and values. You might be able to smooth the waters by reminding employees often that they're working toward the same goals and have to figure out how to do so harmoniously.

Workplace conflict can be difficult and counterproductive, and should be taken seriously in order to avoid a loss of productivity and possible morale problems.

Why You Need to Follow Up

I touched on the importance of following up on performance problems a few pages back, but further explanation is warranted because not doing so could have negative consequences.

You can't know if the performance gap has been fixed without paying attention and monitoring the situation. Nor will you know if additional problems crop up. Just as important, an employee who makes a big effort to correct a problem, only to have the effort go unnoticed, is not an employee who will be eager to boost his or her performance. Let's take a closer look.

To Monitor Whether the Situation Improves

You addressed the matter of the mail not being picked up on time with Jack, and you helped him come up with a plan to make sure that his performance improved and that he met expectations concerning the mail.

Failing to follow up on the situation takes away the influence you have in making sure that the situation does indeed improve. Jack will be much more likely to carry through with his plan for improvement and to be consistent with his efforts if he knows you're monitoring the situation.

Once he becomes used to collecting the mail in a manner that ensures timely pickup, it will become a habit, and you can look at how to boost his performance level even more.

To Address Additional Problems

Just because Jack is now on track with collecting the mail on time doesn't mean you can assume there will be no other problems. Sometimes solving one performance problem can actually lead to another one. What if Jack is so determined to get the mail collected on time that he neglects another job task that needs to be done during the time he's designated for mail pickup? He's solved one problem, but it resulted in another.

Or an unrelated problem could pop up, and you won't know about it if you aren't keeping in touch and following through with Jack. Managers need to be constantly on the lookout for what's going on within their departments.

To Recognize Improvement

Employees too often complain that managers are quick to come down on them when a problem occurs but are silent regarding their efforts to solve it and get their performances back on track. All too often, they're right.

It's tempting to want to move on to the next issue once a performance problem has been resolved. You'd like to breathe a sigh of relief, give yourself a pat on the back for addressing the problem, and move on to the next big (or little) thing.

Failing to thank employees for their efforts and recognize the improvement they've made is counterproductive and won't motivate your employees or keep them excited and moving ahead. Recognizing improvement in an employee's performance doesn't take a lot of time or effort, and the results of doing so will be worth it.

The Least You Need to Know

- Most performance gaps can be addressed and improved or solved, but you've got to first recognize a performance problem in order to fix it.
- Don't assume that you know the reason for the performance gap.
- Charge the employee with owning the problem and how to fix it.
- Follow up and follow through to make sure change happens.

In This Chapter

- Identifying a difficult employee
- Recognizing signs of problem behavior
- Dealing with serious behavior problems
- Taking steps to deal with difficult employees
- Following through to make the change happen

Almost every organization has at least one difficult employee, and some have many. These are the workers who don't show up on time, they are hard to get along with, snap at customers, or gossip incessantly about their co-workers—you know what I'm talking about.

While one or two difficult associates can usually be managed easily enough, more than that can cause enough disruption to affect productivity and cause all kinds of trouble. These workers can be especially troublesome if they deal with customers in a sales or other capacity or represent the company outside of its walls.

In this chapter, you'll learn how to recognize these difficult employees early, before they become too disruptive or counterproductive. You'll also discover how to handle them in order to keep your organization running smoothly.

How to Recognize a Difficult Employee

You might think it's easy to recognize a difficult employee, and often it is. Sometimes, however, difficult employees behave in subtle ways that can make it hard to figure out what's going on.

In-your-face difficult employees are easy to recognize. These are the workers who complain out loud to anyone who will listen—including you. They might simply refuse to perform a job you ask them to do. They make no attempt to meet expectations, much less exceed them. They show up late for work. They call in a lot, or maybe just don't show up at all, without giving you the courtesy of a phone call. They might be rude to customers or co-workers or management. These kinds of employees cause problems, but at least they're easily recognizable problems. Their behaviors make it easy to identify them as problem employees, giving you the opportunity to deal with them quickly and keep the situation in hand.

More difficult to recognize are employees who act like everything is fine and they're happy to be performing their jobs when, actually, they're undermining your efforts and the efforts of your team. These employees are sometimes referred to as "toxic" employees. They're the ones who gossip and spread rumors about co-workers or managers, and complain about you behind your back to other employees or, even worse, customers. They refuse to be involved with or engaged in the workplace. They might be employees who ask co-workers to make excuses for their absences by saying they're visiting clients when they're actually visiting boyfriends or girlfriends. They might tell you they've followed up on all their sales calls, while really following up on just two or three.

PERFORMANCE GAP

While it's tempting to ignore problem behavior and hope it will go away, it's extremely counterproductive and can produce dangerous results. Chances are, a negative situation within a workplace won't resolve itself—at least, not without causing some harm along the way. Ignoring a situation usually allows it to worsen, and that can have serious negative effects on employee morale and productivity, affecting the entire organization.

If a problem employee is acting in an unacceptable manner behind your back, other employees will likely notice the behavior before you do. In fact, you could be completely unaware of the problem behavior, even as other team members become demoralized or start adopting problem behaviors of their own. Toxic behavior has a tendency to spread, like a cold or virus.

That's why it's important to remain alert to signs of problem behavior and act quickly when necessary. Some warning signals of problem behavior include these:

- Whispering or conversation that stops suddenly when you appear

- Small clusters of the same employees who gather often

- An employee who "gets sick" and has to leave work more often than what might be reasonably expected

- Increased arguing between co-workers

- Antagonistic employee behavior

- Aggressive employee behavior, either overtly or passively

- Increased number of negative remarks made by an employee

- Unwillingness of an employee to do anything extra

- Evidence of an employee encouraging others to adopt negative behavior

Recognizing troublesome behavior early is important, because it allows you to act quickly. You need to control it and keep it from affecting other workers. Once you've addressed the situation and worked with the employee to change it, you'll need to reassess to see if improvement has occurred. If it has not, it's probably time for disciplinary action or perhaps dismissal.

How to Handle Difficult Employees

Difficult employees come in many flavors, but the manner in which you handle them should be pretty standard. Of course you'll need to handle each employee a little differently, depending on each one's personality and temperament, but basically, there's a formula to working with problem employees. You'll recognize some of these steps from the FEW method introduced in Chapter 9. The FEW method advises that you state the *facts* regarding the performance problem, share the *effects* the performance problem has caused, and ask *why* the problem has occurred.

The formula for handling difficult employees includes a few additional steps:

1. Identify the problem behavior.

2. Let the employee know that you recognize the behavior.

3. Explain the impact of the negative behavior.

4. Ask the employee to share the reason for the behavior.

5. Restate your expectations of the employee.

6. Work with the employee to come up with a plan for correcting the behavior and getting back on track with the job.

Let's take a look at some specific forms of problem behavior and walk through some scenarios of how you might address those types of employees.

Boredom

A bored employee can exhibit problem behavior, but this often isn't really a problem employee. Boredom is easily remedied, and these employees normally are easy to get back on track.

If Beth has taken to chatting constantly with the people around her, checking her personal e-mail often, and spending time on Facebook during work hours, she could have too much time on her hands because she's bored with her work.

If you suspect that's the case, call her on the behavior and see if you're right. Once you've confirmed the cause for her behavior, explain to her that the constant chatting is causing other employees to fall behind on their work, and Beth's personal screen time is detracting from the overall productivity of the organization.

In the case of a bored employee, you don't need to restate the expectations you've established; you need to establish new expectations. Beth needs to be challenged in order to eliminate the boredom factor, so expectations need to be enhanced.

PERFORMANCE BOOST

If you notice a sudden change in an employee's behavior, act on it immediately to find out why. There's always a reason for a behavior change, and the faster you can determine what's going on, the easier it will be to work with the employee to facilitate improvement.

You might increase her work quantitatively by asking her to make 30 calls a day instead of 20. She might respond to a completely different type of job within the organization or be inspired by being asked to handle greater responsibility. Involve Beth by asking what you can do to make her job more interesting and to help her increase her productivity. Work together to generate a plan on how she'll improve her behavior.

Laziness

Some employees will always try to get away with achieving the least amount of work possible. They simply can't be bothered to do anything extra, and they may whine and complain when asked to.

This type of behavior, of course, is unfair to other employees, who often end up doing more than their share to make up for the lazy employees. As a manager, you need to intervene for the sake of not only the underachieving employee, but the rest of the team as well.

When notifying a lazy employee that his problem behavior needs to change, be sure to talk only about the behavior, not the employee's personal characteristic of laziness.

> **PERFORMANCE BOOST**
>
> When dealing with a difficult employee, keep your conversation as positive as possible, and focus only on the employee's behavior. Think back to your Psychology 101 course, where you probably learned that it's better to start a sentence with *I* than *you*. Say, "I've noticed that you've been having some trouble completing your work" instead of "You're holding the department back because you haven't been completing your work." Putting the focus on you can keep the employee from getting defensive or shutting down because he or she perceives you're in attack mode. And be sure to provide feedback so the employee knows you're listening to what he or she has to say.

Also be sure to point out the results the employee's actions have on the rest of the team and the business in general. If Ryan fails to clean out and rearrange the stock in the walk-in cooler, the workers who stock the cooler after the delivery truck comes have to shift the product around in order to get the stuff that has to be sold first to the front. That doubles their work and puts them behind on their work schedule. Once Ryan understands the impact that his actions have on co-workers, he may be more open to working harder so he doesn't inconvenience them.

When dealing with this type of employee, you need to review the expectations you've established and ask the worker to come up with a plan for how to meet them. Deal with lazy workers as soon as the problem becomes apparent, for they can negatively affect the morale of co-workers. The last thing you want is even the perception among other workers that you're letting a lazy employee get away with problem behavior.

Chip on the Shoulder

No manager enjoys working with employees who have a chip on their shoulder, but, as you know, it comes with the territory. The first thing you need to do is address the problem with the employee.

You can say something like, "Courtney, I notice that you don't seem very happy here lately. Can you tell me what's going on?"

It's important to identify the reason for the problem behavior before trying to deal with a difficult employee, and you can't assume that you know what it is. Maybe Courtney's workload has increased significantly. If her negative attitude has become apparent since the extra work was added, you might be tempted to assume that she's upset about that, when actually she's dealing with a bad situation at home. Allow her to tell you what's going on, and together, figure out how to accommodate or solve the problem.

CASE IN POINT

Everybody, including Stu, thought he'd be happy when he was promoted from a machine operator to supervisor of the tool crib. It turned out that everybody, including Stu, was wrong. Stu hated having to manage equipment and the people who used it, and he badly missed the routine of his old job. The trouble was, instead of talking about it, Stu developed a giant chip on his shoulder as he went about doing the job he so disliked. When his manager finally confronted him, he was able to talk about the problem, which was solved by letting Stu go back to his machine.

Unwillingness to Change

These employees can be a big problem because sometimes seniority is accompanied by a sense of privilege or a feeling that the rules don't apply.

Steve, a long-time employee, balked loudly about having to install a new software program. It wasn't necessary, he said; the current program worked just fine. His manager had to explain to Steve that although the current program seemed to be sufficient, it would not support the new customer service initiatives the company was working to implement. Increased competition and customer expectations made it necessary to upgrade the software program.

Again, you need to address the issue with the problem employee and explain the consequences of his behavior. Explain that if the new program isn't up and running by the middle of the next month, other employees won't be able to track customer orders or keep customers informed of the status. Also point out that, during the employee's long tenure, Steve has been a part of many changes within the organization. Workers sometimes forget these inconvenient truths.

Once Steve agrees to install the software program, be sure to continue the discussion until you're satisfied that he understands the impact that his behavior has on other workers and the entire organization.

Unwillingness to Take On More Responsibility

An employee may be reluctant to accept additional responsibility for a number of reasons. Jean could already feel overwhelmed and honestly doesn't feel capable of doing any more work than she's already doing. Or her responsibilities at home or elsewhere in her life have increased and she's reluctant to add to that burden. Again, the best way to find out what's going on is to ask her.

Maybe Jean lacks the confidence necessary to take on additional responsibility, or maybe some aspect of the extra work is uncomfortable to her. If the additional responsibility would require her to greet customers as they enter the store and she's an extremely shy person, for instance, she might not be looking to avoid additional work—she's just really uncomfortable with some aspect of that work.

Together you and the employee can decide whether the expectations in place can be changed to accommodate additional responsibility that the employee can comfortably handle or whether the employee should move to a different area.

PERFORMANCE GAP

One of the worst things a manager can do is to rely on second-hand information about an employee. If you hear from Lori that Sarah Ann is upset because she was scheduled to work this weekend but it's actually Donavan's weekend to work, don't assume that you understand the scenario. You might have noticed that Sarah Ann is upset, but it might have nothing to do with the weekend shift; Lori might have passed along information that was completely inaccurate. Go to the source of the problem to find out what's going on, or risk having your respect level diminished.

Desire to Coast Toward Retirement

I suppose that coasting toward retirement has occurred as long as employees have been retiring, but it doesn't justify the behavior. If you encounter this type of problem employee, it's your job to call out that behavior and, again, explain the impact it has on other workers and the company. Say that as long as this person is an employee, the company expects him or her to meet the established expectations, and then review the expectations together. Let the employee come up with a plan for getting back on track and remaining a productive member of the team until retirement.

A Problem Employee—or a Dangerous One?

There's a huge difference between an employee who is bored or unmotivated while coasting toward retirement and one who is actually a danger to others or the operation of your business. Recognizing dangerous behavior is the responsibility of a manager, and you must be prepared to do so. Make sure you know the company's policy regarding serious workplace issues such as violence, drug or alcohol use, stealing, bullying, and sexual harassment. If you observe or learn of any of these behaviors, they'll need to be addressed immediately, according to company policy. Many companies have established "zero tolerance" policies for serious offenses; if that's the case, you'll need to follow through. However, if you did not actually observe the behavior, be certain that it did occur. Remember to document all observations, actions, and people involved.

If you suspect or know that a dangerous situation involving violence is pending or imminent, contact law enforcement officials immediately and follow workplace policies for protecting employees.

Making Sure That Change Happens

You probably noticed that these scenarios for dealing with problem employees had many similarities, based on the following steps:

1. Identifying the problem behavior

2. Letting the employee know you're aware of the behavior

3. Explaining the impact of the behavior

4. Asking the employee to share the reason for the behavior

5. Restating your expectations for the employee

6. Working with the employee to come up with a plan for change

Those steps don't always occur in the same order, and you may not use them all in every situation. Still, they are a good foundation for addressing problem employees.

Addressing a problem, however, is not the same as solving it. If Steve, the long-time employee who was reluctant to install the new software program, agrees to do the work, does the work, and then reverts back to his habit of complaining about change and balking at doing what needs to be done to support that change, you're left with the same problem you had—and it may be more difficult to deal with the next time a situation occurs.

I like the saying "Nice words don't cook rice." This means, of course, that employees can say whatever they like, but if they (and you) don't follow through, necessary change won't happen. Steve can apologize for giving you a hard time, acknowledge that he understands why change is necessary, and assure you that he'll work harder and keep up with everything new that comes along, but, if he doesn't do it, those are just nice words that won't cook rice.

A big part of the formula for dealing with problem employees is to, together, come up with a plan for solving the problem behavior. And just as you were advised to do in Chapter 9, which focused on dealing with performance problems, you need to follow up to make sure the behavior changes. Once you and your employee have come up with a plan of action that includes measurable behaviors within time frames, it's your job to verify that those desirable behaviors occur. If they don't, you might have to employ disciplinary action or consider terminating employment.

CASE IN POINT

Christine was a problem employee for several reasons. She did the absolute minimum amount of work required, refused to stay a minute past 5:30, spent far too much time checking gossip websites, and bristled at the faintest hint of criticism. Her manager had called her on her behavior numerous times, including after observing her playing computer games when she should have been working. Every time, Christine would cry and make excuses, promise to change, and then revert right back to the problem behaviors. At some point, it becomes necessary to decide whether putting up with that kind of behavior is worth it; if not, it's time to say goodbye to the problem employee. It's not easy, but it's the smart thing to do.

Following up to make sure change occurs can be as simple as walking around and observing an employee's behavior, or making the employee accountable through reporting of tasks accomplished and so forth.

Schedule follow-up meetings with problem employees to evaluate and discuss whether the plans for meeting stated expectations are staying on track or need to be readdressed. Let employees have their say, and if there are valid reasons for why the expectations can't be met, listen to and address those reasons.

Every good manager knows that employees are valuable commodities. You and the company invest a lot of time, money, and energy in every worker, and once they're on board it's usually desirable to retain employees unless the situation is not repairable or begins degrading the goals of other employees and the organization.

Employees who cause problems shouldn't automatically be let go, because they could turn out to be star performers. Until you understand what's causing the problem behavior and come up with a plan for fixing it, try to be patient with these workers—but never at the expense of the rest of your team.

The Least You Need to Know

- Recognizing problem employees isn't always easy.
- Address problem behavior quickly once it's apparent.
- Certain actions are necessary when dealing with problem employees, but you should always directly involve the employee.
- Make sure policies are in place to address serious behaviors.
- Follow up with employees to make sure change occurs and the behavior doesn't reoccur.

Tools for Boosting Performance

Part

3

Interaction with employees is vital, whether they're brand new or seasoned performers. Part 3 deals with the training and development necessary for boosting performance, starting on day one. You'll learn how to improve performance with performance action plans, and you'll discover why customer contact and feedback is vital to your business and the success of your employees.

Bring New Employees

In This Chapter

- Orientation for all employees
- Why the first 90 days are critical
- Setting the tone for employment from day one
- Checking in after 90 days

Finding and hiring new employees can be both time-consuming and expensive. That means once you've made a hire, you want your new employee to be up and running in as little time as possible. You also want to ensure that the new employee will be successful in his new position.

Most managers agree that 90 days is about what it takes for an employee to become integrated as part of the team, with enough knowledge and experience to be effective at his job. A common and often costly mistake is to launch new employees into independence too early, before they've had time to get comfortable with the work they'll be doing, or even before they have a full understanding of the goals and mission of the company.

There's no magic formula to a 90-day onboarding, or the process of integrating a new employee, but 3 months seems to be about the time you should expect it to take for an employee to be trained, comfortable, and ready to work independently.

New to the Company or New to the Position?

Orientation is necessary for both employees who are new to the company and those who are changing positions within the company. Managers often assume that an employee who's been around for a while can easily hop from one job to another with little or no disruption to productivity, but that's not necessarily the case.

It's true that an employee moving from one job to another within your organization already has knowledge that a new employee would not possess. She has an understanding of the goals and mission of the company, is familiar with the culture of the company, and knows where the lunchroom is and how the coffee machine works. As far as the new job goes, however, that employee requires the same training as an employee just coming into the company.

CASE IN POINT

Jasmine was the receptionist in a busy government office. Personable and articulate, she handled the phones and walk-in clients like a real pro. So when a caseworker's position opened, Jasmine was offered the job, shown to her desk, given a brief overview of her duties, and left on her own. Everyone expected Jasmine to jump in and handle her new position with the same level of proficiency she'd exhibited at the front desk, even though she had not been given nearly enough orientation or training. This, of course, was extremely unfair to Jasmine, because it set her up to fail. To her credit, she spoke up and eventually was given the necessary training for her to succeed.

When employees move from one position to another, they should receive the same considerations as a new employee, and the process by which they will be trained for the position should be established and expressed. Employees need to know that you consider the move they're making to be important and that these employees aren't afterthoughts to the hiring process.

You'll need to re-establish job performance standards and expectations for an employee's new job and explain how the position fits into the overall operation of the company. You won't need to explain how the coffee machine works, review work hours and break schedules, or talk about parking, but, other than that, you should treat a worker in a new position within your organization pretty much the same as a brand-new employee.

Why 90 Days?

As I said earlier, there's nothing magic about a 90-day orientation period, but neither is it a completely arbitrary time frame. For most new employees, the first few days at a new job are confusing and can be disorienting. They don't know the process of the workplace—that is, how things work the way they do and why. Often they're reluctant to ask too many questions because they feel they're being bothersome or intrusive.

PERFORMANCE BOOST

Even seasoned employees who have been in the workplace for a long time can feel disoriented and lost during the first few days or weeks of a new job. It's difficult for a worker to move from the level of competency he possessed in his old job to a level of incompetence he'll temporarily experience in a new job. Managerial patience is a necessity with all new employees.

During the time the employee is trying to get acclimated to the workplace, his new co-workers and managers, a different schedule, and changed job expectations, he's also expected to be learning the job for which he was hired. It's unrealistic to think that effective job education and workplace acclimation can occur in less than 30 days.

The next 30 days provide a time for the new employee to get settled in the job and become a productive and contributing member of the team. That's not to say there should be no expectations of the employee during the first month of hire, but you should observe a new level of comfort and productivity between days 30 and 60.

During the 60- to 90-day period, you'll get a feel for how the new employee is doing and how he's fitting in with the company and other employees. He'll know that there will be a review at the end of 90 days, and both you and he should be preparing for that. That review gives you and the new employee a chance to discuss strengths and areas in which changes might be necessary.

So while 90 days isn't set in stone—some employees can be comfortably integrated in 45 days, while others will require considerably more time—count on about 90 days for a new worker to be up to speed and a fully contributing member of your team. Performance boosting, however, can begin on day one.

The First 30 Days

An employee's first day of work is crucial, as are the days that follow. The employee will probably be nervous, self-conscious, and unsure. Don't ever make the mistake of showing new employees to their office or work area and leaving them on their own to fill out forms or review policy sheets.

Some steps to take and tasks to get out of the way on your new employee's first day include the following:

- Lay out the plans for that day and the next few days. A new employee is likely to be nervous, and knowing what to expect can alleviate some anxiety.

- Get other employees on board for welcoming a new worker. Make sure she meets all the employees with whom she'll be working directly, as well as any others that she might need to have contact with. Don't forget other managers and higher-ups. If you're a small organization or the new employee will be a part of a small team, consider arranging a welcome lunch on the first day, to give her a chance to meet her co-workers.

- Remind other employees to be mindful of helping the new worker and anticipating any questions or problems he might have.

- Handle the administrative stuff. If your company doesn't have a human relations department, going over contracts, benefits packages, and other important paperwork may fall on you. This may make you a little impatient, especially if it's your job with every new employee, but remember that it's critical to the employee.

- Talk about conditions of employment, including a probationary period and when and how evaluations are conducted. Go over any company rules and regulations.

- Show the employee the organizational chart for the department or company, and let her know how she fits in. Discuss her job and how it contributes to the bigger picture of overall company goals. Make it a point to be positive and motivating.

- Show him around. It's really important for a new employee to have a sense of his surroundings, especially if the organization is divided, such as offices and a manufacturing facility. Don't forget to point out common areas such as restrooms and the coffee or break room.

- Cover the little stuff if she doesn't already know. Where should she park? What's the Internet policy? What if she needs supplies? How long is her lunch break? Where's a good, quick place to grab a sandwich? Are there certain stairs or doors she shouldn't use? It's easy to overlook basic concerns of new workers, but they won't know if somebody doesn't tell them.

- Establish your supervisory relationship. Spending time with a new employee in the very first days of hiring gives you a chance to get to know him and to establish your relationship. He'll get a sense of your management style, and you'll get a sense of his interest in the position and the company, his background, and his aspirations.

PERFORMANCE BOOST

It's perfectly normal for even the greatest employees to be nervous on the first day. In fact, I'd wonder about a new employee who didn't have some butterflies on the first day! New employees are uncertain regarding just about everything, which can result in feelings of being overwhelmed. One of the most important things you can do for a new employee is to let him know what to expect and assure him that you and other members of the team are available and willing to help him get up to speed.

It's extremely important on day one that an employee be properly welcomed, introduced to all applicable co-workers, and made familiar with the nuts and bolts of how the organization works. This lays a firm foundation for learning and becoming proficient at the job, and it sets the stage for success.

Educate

Ideally, all your workers should be learning new skills and acquiring new information every day they're on the job. A new worker, however, requires intentional, thought-out education concerning not only the actual job, but many other aspects of the workplace as well.

Most offices, stores, and plants are busy places. Workplaces that have downsized employees are particularly busy, and you might think that taking your time or the time of another employee to educate a new hire is frivolous or bothersome. Some managers think that a new hire should be able to buddy up with another employee and learn the job by watching and asking some questions. Many employees might actually be able to do that. The problem with this approach, however, is that, without any sort of formal training, it could take longer for the new employee to learn the job, and if the "teaching" employee has any bad habits or other shortcomings, the new hire may pick them up.

PERFORMANCE GAP

If you designate another employee to show a new worker around or perform other onboarding tasks, choose that employee with care. The last thing you want is for an employee who's unhappy with his or her job to give a new employee an earful about perceived faults of the company. That can undermine any other orientation you attempt.

Also, the manager is the one who needs to establish and communicate job performance standards and expectations, and make sure they're understood and documented. Educating a new hire about expectations to meet is as important as providing on-the-job training, and you may be the only person who's able to supply that education.

New employees who are educated quickly and thoroughly will be empowered employees, with the knowledge and confidence necessary to step up and perform their jobs effectively. They'll become contributing team members far more quickly than they would without adequate education about the job—and this benefits everyone.

Equip

Make sure new employees have all the tools and equipment necessary to perform the job effectively. Do they need office supplies? A uniform? A company car? A laptop? A company e-mail address? Business cards?

If you're not certain what supplies or equipment is necessary, check with another employee in a similar position. Make a checklist, if necessary, and encourage the new hire to ask for anything else needed. Introduce the employees to the person in charge of supplies.

Equipment also can come in the form of assistance, support, and backup, so make sure new hires are well supplied in those areas as well.

Immerse

An employee who is quickly immersed in a job is likely to become more invested and interested in that job than one who is introduced to a position gradually. Therefore, the more time you or another person can spend getting the employee up to speed and acclimated during the first 30 days, the greater the chances are that the new hire will quickly become a highly functioning member of the team. This requires an investment of time and effort up front, but immersing a new hire in the job and the company has definite benefits.

Check In

During the first 30 days, check in often with new employees, or have them check in often with you. Make it a point to review job performance expectations and make sure they are understood, and to ask whether workers have any questions or concerns.

These check-ins don't need to be formal or even announced. You can perform a check-in simply by stopping by a new employee's desk or work area and asking a few questions. Don't ask vague questions to which the employee can give a vague answer. Instead of asking, "How's it going?" you can ask, "Tell me about yesterday when you processed your first customer claim. What steps did you use to do that?" Likewise, instead of asking, "Is everything going okay?", you could say something like, "I've noticed that you seem to have a little trouble with the equipment at one point of the production process. How about we get Darren to go over that step with you?"

PERFORMANCE BOOST

Although you should check in frequently with your new employee, you might also consider scheduling a more formal meeting at the end of the first 30 and 60 days, to provide feedback and give the new hire a chance to talk about any problems or concerns. The 30- and 60-day reviews won't be as comprehensive as the one after 90 days, but they're a good means of developing good communication with your new worker.

Be specific and open with your new employees, and encourage them to be open with you. New employees often paint a rosy picture even when things are not going so well because they want to make a good impression. It's far better to get an accurate picture of accomplishments and challenges early on, to avoid potential problems.

Take notes on what you observe so you can refer back to them before a more formal review. Resist the temptation to believe that you'll remember every observation you make and every conversation you have with your new hire.

The 30- to 90-Day Period

Most employees will be feeling pretty comfortable in a job after the first 30 days. Sure, they still have a lot to learn, but new hires should at least be comfortable with the basics and reasonably settled in. Hopefully, they're feeling comfortable with their co-workers and are fitting into the culture of the company. You and your new employees also should have time by the end of 30 days to establish a working relationship.

The next 60 days, the 30- to 90-day period, is no less important than the initial start time, for this is when you'll begin to see the real deal. When they're comfortable with their surroundings and acclimated within the company and co-workers, new employees begin to really settle into the job.

As the manager, you need to observe carefully during this time frame to make sure that new employees are on the right track and that their performance is improving. If that's the case, you need to be affirming and encouraging, while still observant of areas that may require attention or improvement.

Some workers, however, make a strong showing when they first start a job and then ease off once they become acclimated and comfortable. The best behavior they were on when they first arrived begins to slide a bit, and the level of interest and cooperation lessens.

Or maybe an employee hasn't learned how to perform the job properly, or doesn't understand the expectations, or simply can't do the job. Any or all of those problems you read about in Chapter 9 can result in performance gaps.

If a new employee isn't meeting job performance expectations, this portion of the orientation period is the time when you need to take action to find out what's going on and what can be done to correct the problem. Not addressing a performance problem during this period is practically guaranteeing the employee an unsuccessful evaluation at the end of the 90-day orientation period.

CASE IN POINT

Tracy had all the right credentials for the customer service representative position at a midsize insurance company. A real go-getter, she showed up to work early and was never in a rush to leave. She was meticulous about completing her call list, well organized, and pleasant. After about three weeks, however, Tracy's manager noticed her performance was slipping. She wasn't as well organized or as enthusiastic, and she started leaving work before she'd returned all the calls she was responsible for. The manager intervened and Tracy was given another chance, but it turned out that her initial work performance had been a show, and she never performed up to that level again. Tracy was dismissed at the end of her 90-day orientation period.

Solicit Questions or Comments

A supervisor should be in close contact with new employees during the entire orientation period, observing and monitoring performance while providing and asking for feedback. You'll need to find out how employees are doing, what they like about the job, and what areas may require some assistance. Ideally, new employees should keep in touch with you, seeking advice or feedback on their performance. Often, however, you'll need to take the initiative.

Many new employees don't ask a lot of questions because they don't want to be a bother or appear to be clueless, so ask often if they have questions about any aspect of the job. Make it clear that, after one or two months, new employees aren't expected to be experts in all facets of the position; let them know that you're accessible and don't mind answering questions. Also ask for feedback about the job and see if they have concerns about any aspect of their work, the work environment, or other topics.

Talk to Other Team Members

The 30- to 90-day period is also the time when you should be checking in with other team members to see how the new employee is working out. These conversations require discretion and sensitivity on your part, of course, but other employees will be able to give you important feedback regarding the new hire. You'll be able to get a sense of how your new hire fits in, her strengths and weaknesses on the job, and whether she seems to be contributing to the goals and mission of the company.

Be sure to keep any queries regarding the new employee general in nature, and stick to conversations about work only—under no circumstances should you engage in conversations that deal with anything of a personal nature.

Day 90 and Beyond

After an employee has been on board for 90 days, you should have a pretty good idea of how he or she is doing. Your frequent check-ins, the notes you've taken, what you've heard from other employees, and discussions between you and your new hire should give you a pretty good picture of how the employee is working out and how the job is going.

Ninety days is typically the length of a new employee's "trial period." Regardless of whether you've conducted performance reviews at 30 and 60 days, you'll definitely want to schedule one for the end of the 90-day period.

The 90-Day Review

You'll learn all about performance reviews in Chapter 15, so we won't spend a lot of time here on the mechanics of conducting a review. Basically, the 90-day review gives you a chance to provide the new employee with feedback about his performance to that point, and to address any areas of concern. You'll want to evaluate general areas such as the following:

- Job competence
- Ability to learn new skills
- Ability to work independently
- Ability to work as part of a group
- Ability to identify and solve problems
- Dependability in terms of punctuality and attendance
- Organizational skills
- Appropriate use of time

Other areas to be evaluated will vary, depending on the type of job and work circumstances. If an employee supervises another, for instance, you'd evaluate her supervisory abilities. If she works with customers, you'd evaluate her effectiveness in that area.

You can grade each category by noting whether the employee exceeds expectations, meets expectations, or requires improvement. During the review, you'll discuss each category and provide feedback on why the employee received those ratings. Any feedback you provide should be positive, fair, and factual, as noted in Chapter 2.

Many managers dislike performance reviews, but they're an integral and necessary part of the performance management cycle, which is key to boosting employee performance. It's important to be prepared for the review and for your new employee to know what to expect. Chapter 15 covers those areas.

Staying on Track

It's tempting after 90 days to assume that a new employee is no longer a new employee and should be performing at 100 percent capacity. When you think about it, though, 90 days isn't a long period in which to learn a new job, get to know a bunch of co-workers, and learn to navigate a new environment. Continue your observation of new employees long after the 90-day period has ended; don't just assume that they are completely up-to-speed in the new job. And remember that when an employee gets settled in and is feeling comfortable in a new position, her productivity sometimes slides a bit.

It's your job to make sure the new employee stays on track and to do whatever you're able to in order to help her meet—and exceed—the performance expectations you've established.

The Least You Need to Know

- The first 90 days are critical to a new employee's success.
- Spending time and energy on a new employee is a wise investment.
- Check in with the new hire frequently during the first 90 days.
- Continue tracking performance even after the 90-day review.

Training and Development

In This Chapter

- Knowing when and how to train
- Getting your money's worth
- The different types of training
- Getting training help

Training isn't the answer to every performance issue, but it certainly has its place and can go a long way in boosting employee performance.

As the second step in the performance management cycle, training should always be provided for new employees and employees moving from one position to another within the organization. However, job training is also an ongoing process that shouldn't be restricted to new workers or those changing jobs.

In this chapter, you'll learn how to determine whether training is necessary and explore some options for providing training. While training can be an excellent tool and a great motivator for employees, it has to make sense for your organization.

How to Know Whether Training Will Work

Training is necessary for employees who don't possess the knowledge and skills necessary to succeed at their jobs. These employees are unable to meet or exceed expectations because they're not equipped to do the work.

If Morgan's job is to maintain the company's computer system and teach co-workers about upgrades and new programs, and twice in the past week he's been unable to diagnose a problem, chances are good that Morgan needs additional training. Maybe the system has changed or Morgan has no experience with some new programs being put into use. If that's the case, additional training is applicable and necessary, because it will enable Morgan to improve his knowledge and skills, and, ultimately, will boost his performance.

This assumes, however, that Morgan's issue is a lack of knowledge. If the issue stems from something else, such as a lack of interest or unwillingness to diagnose problems, all the training in the world won't boost his performance. Or perhaps Morgan knows how to do the work but doesn't understand what he's supposed to be doing. That's a communication issue, not a training issue. In that case, you need to provide Morgan with feedback regarding what you expect of him, and make sure that he acknowledges and fully understands those expectations.

CASE IN POINT

Tameka worked at the cosmetics counter in an upscale department store. A happy, experienced employee, she was doing great until the store installed a new computer system. At checkout, the system gathered information on shopper preference and inventory for company headquarters. Tameka seemed to have a terrible time with the new electronics and, as a result, became less personable with customers. They started complaining about their service. Tameka's manager spent some time with her and realized the issue wasn't that Tameka couldn't learn the new system—she resented having to learn it and had no interest in learning it. No amount of training could have helped the unwilling Tameka.

In short, training will work if employees require additional knowledge or skills to do their assigned jobs. It won't work if employees are falling short due to other issues, such as these:

- Unwillingness to work

- Failure to understand expectation

- Excessive absenteeism

- Poor work habits

- Too many distractions

- Personal problems that detract from job performance

Employees who lack knowledge or skills will almost always be receptive to training. Some will even ask for it. If a lack of skills or knowledge is the cause of the work problem and the employee isn't receptive to training, the issue becomes one of unwillingness to work at meeting expectations.

What Kind of Training Is Best?

If Morgan needs help learning a difficult new software product, you want to find the right type and source of training for him. You don't want to waste time and money sending him to a three-day seminar covering topics he'll never encounter in his daily work life. You just want to get him trained so he's comfortable with the software program necessary for him to do his job effectively.

You could send him to a three-day course at a computer consulting firm, or buy an online tutorial and give Morgan time off to use it and learn the program. All types of training programs and options are available, and you'll read more about them later in this chapter. When determining the type of training necessary, use the practical steps outlined next.

Look Around You

Take a good look around your workplace and observe what's going on. Do your employees appear to be busy? Are they focused on their work, or do they seem distracted? Is anyone looking uncertain about what they're doing or asking someone else for help?

If Courtney isn't getting the reports she's responsible for filed on time, observe her to see why. Does it appear that she's using her time wisely, or is she checking e-mail and text-messaging? Does she seem to have trouble understanding how the reports are to be done? Does she understand the time frame in which they need to be done?

If she's having trouble managing her time, perhaps she needs some training on time-management skills. If she doesn't understand how to do the reports, she needs training on filling out forms and writing reports. If she doesn't understand the time frame in which the work is to be completed, she probably doesn't require training; an explanation of expectations should be satisfactory.

For some reason, managers often don't take advantage of the powerful tool of simple observation. You can learn a lot by keeping your eyes open and watching your employees in action.

Ask Your Employee

An employee who is experiencing job difficulty likely knows better than anyone what sort of training would be most beneficial. If Greg is having trouble learning how to use the new phone system, ask him whether he'd prefer to have someone sit with him and walk him through the different features of the system, or whether he'd prefer to spend time by himself with the printed information. Or perhaps he'd like to call the provider's help desk to discuss the problematic aspects of the system.

> **PERFORMANCE BOOST**
>
> Remember that you may have training resources among your own staff members. Consider asking an employee who's adept at a certain task to provide some training for another employee who is struggling with that task.

Remember that not everyone shares the same learning style, and the type of training that works best for one employee might not work best for another. Some people learn better by listening, while others do better when they read instructions. Some employees are more comfortable with group training and like to brainstorm with others and share questions and idea; others prefer solitary, online training that allows them to move at their own pace.

Asking employees who are experiencing a problem to consider what type of training might be useful also gives them a chance to talk to you about the problem. Make sure employees know you're willing to provide the help they need to get back on track.

Use Your Own Experience

If you've moved up through the ranks to your current position, think about training that you would have found useful in your past jobs. Have you always wished you'd learned more about how the orders you received from customers were handled after they left your desk? Maybe the employees currently handling customer orders would benefit from the same type of training.

Do you recall that once after a promotion you were left floundering because you hadn't received the proper training for your new responsibilities? Or are you still uncertain about parts of the company's distribution process because you never were thoroughly trained? Using your own experience, put yourself in your employees' positions and determine what type of training is desirable and necessary.

> **PERFORMANCE BOOST**
>
> Assess each of your employees and the work individuals are doing. Then ask yourself, "When I was first in that job (or a similar position), what training would have helped me to do it better?" Training that helped you, or perhaps wasn't provided but would have helped you, most likely will benefit your employees as well.

Check Out Your Performance Reviews

You're going to read a lot more about performance reviews in Chapter 15, but they apply to this chapter in that they may contain answers to the type of training you should provide to your employees.

Many performance reviews contain a development section in which managers suggest training to boost performance. Check out the last couple reviews for an employee you think might need some training, and you just might find suggestions on the type of training that will most benefit him or her.

If the review doesn't contain a development section, look over the rest of the document carefully. Chances are, some information within the review will indicate training that will help boost your employee's performance.

How to Define and Measure Results of Training

Training an employee involves time, effort, and expense, so you'll want to make sure you see results from the efforts you make.

When providing training for an employee, you'll first want to clearly state what the employee needs to be trained to do better and then measure the results of the training. This involves using a variety of criteria, which you need to identify. Are you looking to reduce the number of customer complaints? Increase an employee's production rate? Perhaps your training goal is simply to observe that your employees now use the correct procedures when performing their jobs.

Results can be measured in many ways, but gauging the outcomes is a necessary part of training employees.

Determine the Purpose of Training

If you don't know why you're recommending an employee for training, there's no point in wasting your organization's time and money. Pursue training when employees lack the knowledge or skills to do their job. The purpose of training, then, is to equip employees to do their jobs effectively by teaching them additional knowledge or skills. When you identify the knowledge or skills that need to be acquired, you've got the purpose for the training. If there's no identifiable purpose, training can't be effective.

Linda was never trained to wait on customers, doesn't know how to wait on customers, and was recently shifted to a position in which she's expected to wait on customers all the time. The purpose of the training Linda will receive, of course, is to teach her how to wait on customers. The training should provide Linda with the knowledge and skills she needs to be able to wait on customers in a professional manner.

PERFORMANCE GAP

Whatever the reason for training, be sure that the employee to be trained knows what it is and understands the purpose of the training. I've seen employees who were placed in training with no understanding of why they're there, or who resent the training because they don't feel that it's necessary. Those employees generally do not emerge from training as more productive and happy employees. You have to determine the purpose of the training, and they determine the outcome.

Measure the Results

If your department recently underwent safety training in response to recent concerns, how will you measure results to determine whether the training was successful? Remember that results can be quantitative, qualitative, and sometimes a combination. If you observe that employees are using the recommended procedures they learned during training and that the number of reported safety incidents has dropped since training was completed, those are measures that the training worked.

The recommended procedures that you observe your employees using are a qualitative measurement and refer to the quality of your employees' behaviors. The decreased number of safety incidents is a quantitative result, referring to the quantity, or number, of reports.

A third measure used to gauge results is time, and it often overlaps with qualitative and quantitative measures. If training resulted in your employees completing their work in less time than they did before training, that is a measure of the training's success.

On the flip side, if your sales department recently underwent customer service training, but the number of customer complaints has actually increased and you don't observe the employees using any of the recommended strategies for dealing with customers, you can assume that the training was not successful. The increased number of complaints is a quantitative measure, while the behavior of your employees' is a qualitative one.

Keep track of any measurable results after training occurs. If the training isn't successful, you'll need to re-evaluate the process and decide whether you want to try again.

Involve Other Employees

Having employees assist in the training of other employees works well in many organizations. Employees who train other employees often are uniquely qualified to help determine whether the training was useful and successful.

Even if you're not having employees actually conduct the training of others on your team, an experienced employee should be able to identify useful types of training, as well as any training that wasn't worthwhile.

Types of Training

Dozens of training methods are available. You can send employees to workshops or seminars, or have consultants come to you. You can get training online, from books, or in classroom settings. Training methods vary greatly, but the first point to consider is whether training will occur on-site or off-site.

Both options have advantages and disadvantages. Some advantages of on-site training include these:

- Training can be customized to meet the needs of your particular organization.
- Training occurs closer to the actual workplace.
- More people can be included in the training.
- Time and expense is reduced.
- Proximity links training to the job.

Some disadvantages of on-site training include these:

- Employees may face distractions from ringing phones, co-workers, and so on.

- Training isn't viewed as "special" or particularly important because it's on-site.

- The workplace may not have adequate facilities for training.

- The workplace may not have all equipment desirable for training.

Advantages of off-site training include these:

- Training is set apart as something important and special.

- Work distractions are minimized.

- You choose the type of environment you want.

- All necessary equipment and supplies are provided.

- You get to view employees in a nonwork environment setting.

Disadvantages of off-site training include these:

- Off-site training typically costs more than on-site training.

- Travel time can cut down on actual training time.

- You may not have a choice of training provider.

- You may not be able to control how training proceeds.

When you've decided whether training will occur on-site or off-site, you can consider different flavors of training.

Self-Study Programs

There is no shortage of self-study programs on practically any topic you can imagine. These programs can be very specific or more general, and range from learning a foreign language, to optimizing memory, to learning how to use software programs. Be sure to read up on a program before you buy it, as quality varies greatly.

Seminars, Webinars, and Workshops

A variety of training companies, schools, and other organizations offer seminars and workshops on topics ranging from strategic management, to basket weaving, to social networking.

These days, you can also get in on webinars, which are Internet-based seminars that can be accessed from the privacy of your office or your company's conference room. The cost and quality of these training venues and programs vary greatly, so you'll need to do some research.

One-on-One Training

One-on-one training never goes out of style, and it continues to be of value in most organizations. You, another employee, or someone else within your company could provide individual training for a worker who needs additional skills or knowledge.

One-on-one training offers many advantages, including the fact that it can be completely personalized to include only the specific training needs of the employee, leaving out unnecessary information.

PERFORMANCE GAP

Beware of employees who balk at career-development and training opportunities. The rate of change in the workplace is ever increasing, and an employee who isn't willing to learn new skills and increase knowledge will drag down your team and possibly the entire organization.

Computer-Based Training

Employees who are working to learn new skills or increase knowledge might find it reassuring to be able to move at their own pace. Computer-based training makes it possible for a worker to learn at a comfortable speed. However, although that feature is often desirable, it may encourage some employees to drag out the training time.

Computer-based training programs are often interactive, allowing the user to "practice" new skills and verify knowledge. A wide range of these training programs are available.

Simulation Training

Simulation training allows employees to perform their jobs, either in person or virtually, within a safe environment. This allows the employee to experience the realities of the job without any associated risks. Airline pilots have traditionally used simulation training, which now is available in a range of applications, including customer service, interview situations, and performance appraisal.

Job Rotation

Performing a job is the best way to learn about it, making job rotation an attractive training option for many organizations. If you choose this option, just be sure that someone is available to help the employee who is being shifted to a new position.

Classroom Training

Training classes are available in just about any topic you can imagine, both at walk-in locations and online. Distance learning is increasingly popular because it enables people to take classes outside of regular work hours. Walk-in classes are a bit more restrictive, but many offer night or weekend classes as well.

Getting Help When You Need It

Many companies don't go outside for help with employee training and instead use qualified people within the organization. As long as you have the facilities, space, and expertise necessary, that type of training is possible.

If you feel that you could use some outside help, however, keep a few points in mind. Training consultants come from a wide variety of backgrounds, and their qualifications can vary tremendously. You can find training consultant firms and organizations, but these also will vary in quality, price, and other factors.

If you live in or near a metropolitan area, you will probably have a selection of consultants to choose from. Probably the best means of finding a consultant is to find out who colleagues in business sectors similar to yours have used. You can learn a lot from colleagues about the value of services provided, cost, what was involved, and so forth. It's best if you can get a couple opinions about the same consultant, and don't neglect to ask a consultant for references just because you've obtained information from a colleague. Taking time to do your homework before hiring will help ensure that you get the results you want and avoid wasting time and money on a trainer who can't fully benefit your employees and your organization.

Qualities to Look For

When selecting an outside training consultant, look for a variety of qualities. First, the person you hire should be a good fit for your organization. You want someone who can mirror the attitudes and culture of your company and, just as important, who knows your business, or at least your business sector, and understands the type of training you require.

A consultant should possess the skills to decide—with your input, of course—what type of training your employees require and also have the skills to effectively deliver the training. In addition, you want a consultant who has a good reputation, is experienced, and can supply client testimonials and recommendations.

Advantages

Hiring an outside training consultant can be advantageous for several reasons. Like it or not, employees tend to pay more attention to someone they don't work with every day. They're likely to be receptive to what a consultant has to say and welcome a fresh approach.

Another advantage an outside consultant brings is fresh eyes and ears. An outsider sometimes can easily view and assess a situation that has long gone unrecognized and unaddressed by those who are close to it.

A good consultant can help employees get on the right track, and then periodically assess the workplace to make sure the situation is stable and moving forward. Many employers and managers appreciate having an outsider's opinions and observations on how their organizations are doing.

What to Watch Out For

Hiring a training consultant can benefit your organization, but it includes some risk as well. When looking to hire a consultant, insist on knowing the person's credentials and checking background information. Consulting qualifications vary greatly, and, unfortunately, it's possible to obtain "credentials" that aren't worth much.

Inquire about the consultant's business background and ask for verification. Anyone can make up a resumé and claim extensive business experience without actually having it. Beware of a training consultant who makes excuses when you ask for recommendations. Any worthwhile consultant should share a client list and provide recommendations.

The decision of whether to hire a training consultant should not be made lightly. If you decide to hire an outside consultant, take care in choosing the right person.

The Least You Need to Know

- Training is valuable to boost knowledge and skills, but it's not always the answer.
- Choose the training that addresses the problem.
- Training comes in many shapes and sizes; first decide whether to hold it on- or off-site, and then choose a method.
- Outside training can be helpful in some instances, but do your homework before hiring a consultant.

Performance Action Plans

In This Chapter

- The accountability factor of performance action plans
- Customizing a plan to your employee
- Getting your employees' input
- Following through

If you have an employee whose performance isn't meeting expectations, and you've tried other means of boosting performance without any success, it might be time to consider a performance action plan.

Performance actions plans, sometimes referred to as "action plans for improving performance," are important tools for managers. These plans make employees accountable for their actions and behaviors in a more formal manner than simply providing feedback after coaching, mentoring, or training.

In this chapter, you'll learn all about performance action plans and why they're often effective in boosting performance when other efforts to do so have not succeeded.

What Is It and When Do You Need One?

A performance action plan may be necessary if you have an employee whose performance is not meeting expectations and you've already attempted other means of boosting performance. The plan states the following:

- What an employee is expected to do
- What the employee is actually doing
- The performance gap resulting from the behavior

It also includes an action plan with dates and standards for measuring results. The point is for the manager and the employee experiencing the performance gap to review the plan separately and then discuss its contents. When they've agreed on a workable plan, both people sign the plan.

After a plan is signed and in place, the employee is accountable for fulfilling the actions stated, and the manager is accountable for following up as specified.

PERFORMANCE BOOST

Coaching and mentoring are helpful and often necessary managerial tools, but the results are sometimes short lived. The beauty of performance action plans is that they hold employees accountable for their actions over a period of time, until their performance has met or exceeded stated expectations.

Before you consider implementing a written plan, use the following checklist to make sure you've already exhausted other recommended options:

- ❑ I have established job performance standards and expectations.
- ❑ I have clearly stated those standards and expectations.
- ❑ I have gotten receipt of communication from my employee.
- ❑ I have provided adequate training to the employee to do the job.
- ❑ I have provided additional or ongoing training to the employee.
- ❑ I have provided ongoing coaching.

❑ I have given the employee feedback on a regular basis.

❑ I have mentored, or had someone else mentor, the employee.

If you're satisfied that you've completed all these steps, but your employee is still not meeting performance expectations, consider implementing a performance action plan.

Before you call in your employee to talk about the plan, you should understand that you're taking a significant step that will send a strong message to the employee. Be advised that, although some employees will find the plan useful and helpful, others may consider it as a negative action on your part. If you get this reaction from an employee, produce the completed checklist of steps you've already taken and explain that the employee's performance must improve for him or her to continue in the position. Help your employee understand that a performance action plan is not a negative action, but an intensive effort to help him or her improve performance and begin meeting expectations.

CASE IN POINT

As a security officer in a large department store, Carlos had twice failed to document the activities of customers who had been suspected of shoplifting. As a result, the shoppers could not be detained, and no charges were ever filed. Carlos's supervisor worked with him repeatedly to try to boost his performance, but Carlos continued to fail to document activity that occurred during his shifts, causing additional problems for co-workers and management. The manager eventually put a performance action plan in place, making Carlos accountable for his performance. Carlos responded well to the plan and said that it reminded him every day what he needed to do and in what manner.

Developing Your Own Performance Action Plan

You can find samples and templates for performance action plans on various websites and in business manuals, but it's probably better to come up with one on your own. Developing your own plan allows you to customize it to address a particular problem or problems you're encountering with your employee.

Some managers balk at the idea of writing their own plans. They're afraid doing so will be too difficult or will take too much time. Keep in mind, however, that if you allow the performance gap to continue, you'll need to either continue dealing with it into the foreseeable future or take measures to replace the employee.

Remember that coming up with a plan is only the first step of the process. Implementing it and following up are the really essential parts in ensuring that a performance action plan will make a difference.

What to Include

As you read at the beginning of the chapter, your performance action plan needs to state a desired performance and an actual performance.

If you're writing a performance action plan for Joan, who hasn't been getting the bakery shelves stocked in a timely fashion, your plan might read something like this:

> Desired Performance: Bakery shelves will be fully stocked by 6 A.M.
>
> Actual Performance: Shelves are not fully stocked until after 6 A.M., sometimes as late as 7 A.M.

After stating the expected and actual performances, you need to state the performance gap:

> Performance Gap: Performance expectations of having the shelves fully stocked by 6 A.M. are not being met.

After you've identified and stated the performance gap, you need to outline an action plan for correcting the problem. This could include a step such as "Begin stocking shelves as soon as one category of baked goods has been completed and packaged."

You designate a deadline for when that behavior must be attained and indicate how outcomes will be measured. If the action will be monitored through a visual check by another employee or manager to make sure that a product is being moved out to the shelves on time, for instance, that should be stated in the plan.

The document should indicate that the plan is directed toward Joan, from you, and note her department and position. It also should contain a statement from Joan indicating that she's willing to work on improving her performance, as stated within the plan, and that she understands that her ability or inability to improve her performance will impact her overall job performance rating. Both you and the employee must sign and date the plan.

Keeping It Simple

Preferably, the action plan should fit on one page, contain simple language, and be easily referred to by you and your employee. Be sure to explain that the plan is not intended to create more work for your employee, but hopefully will help him or her improve the work that has not been performed in a satisfactory manner.

PERFORMANCE GAP

The nature of a performance action plan is to address one or two problem areas in a rather general manner. Resist the temptation to include a lot of small and specific behaviors, because that can easily overwhelm the plan and the employee it's intended to help. If there are more than a couple of problem areas to be addressed, you might be beyond a performance action plan with that particular employee and need to consider stronger action, such as letting him or her go.

Writing and talking about the plan in a clear, concise manner makes it seem less threatening to the employee and ensures that both parties clearly understand its contents.

Sample Plan

The following sample performance action plan addresses a problem in the bakery of a regional supermarket chain store. A bakery employee responsible for making sure that bakery shelves were fully stocked by 6 A.M. was not meeting job expectations. The plan, which was put in place for the bakery employee, addresses that performance gap.

Performance Action Plan

Date: May 19, 2010

To: Joan Myers

From: Kevin Foster

Department: Bakery

Desired Performance: Bakery shelves will be fully stocked by 6 A.M.

Actual Performance: Shelves are not fully stocked until after 6 A.M., sometimes as late as 7 A.M.

Performance Gap: Performance expectations of having the shelves fully stocked by 6 A.M. are not being met.

Action: Will have all baked items ready for packaging by 5 A.M.

Deadline: June 1

Measurement: Bakery supervisor will check on and document readiness.

Action: Will begin stocking shelves as soon as one category of baked goods is finished and packaged.

Deadline: June 1

Measurement: Bakery supervisor will make sure shelves are stocked as categories of baked goods are finished and packaged.

Action: Will have bakery shelves fully stocked by 6 A.M.

Deadline: June 1

Measurement: Bakery supervisor will assess the shelves.

I am willing to work toward the goals established above in order to boost my job performance. I will document my progress and report to you regularly to discuss the results. I understand that the results of this plan will factor into my overall job performance evaluation.

Joan Myers (employee signature)   Date:_____

Kevin Foster (manager approval)   Date:_____

Getting Buy-In from Your Employees

A crucial aspect of a successful performance action plan is getting employee buy-in before the plan is implemented. I've known managers who generate action plans and present them to their employees without ever giving the employees opportunities for input. Then those managers wonder why their employees resist putting the plans into place.

Although you don't want to spend hours sitting with an employee hashing over what a performance action plan should include, you shouldn't try to push a plan through without any input from your team member.

The best approach is to come up with a general action plan and present it to the employee, giving the person ample time to look it over before you ask him or her to sign it. Ask if the employee has any ideas for improving the plan, whether anything else should be included in the plan that's not already there, and whether he or she thinks the plan is reasonable and doable.

Offering an employee input into the plan gives that person a sense of ownership and encourages him or her to buy into it. When that happens, the employee will be far more likely to diligently follow the terms of the plan and boost his or her performance.

PERFORMANCE GAP

One of the behaviors employees resent most is their employers making decisions that directly affect them without consulting them first. Even if they have no choice in the matter, employees appreciate getting advance warning and having the matter explained to them. Don't make the mistake of not consulting an employee regarding a performance action plan. You're likely to end up with a resentful, bitter employee if you do.

Following Up on the Performance Action Plan

After writing a plan, reviewing it with your employee, and agreeing that it's workable, it's time to implement and, just as important, follow up on it.

Implementing the plan simply requires you and your employee to agree on a starting date, which probably should be immediately, unless there's a good reason to delay it. Following up on the plan requires a little more commitment.

When the plan is in place, you and your employee should meet regularly to review it and assess whether improvement is being made. Regular check-ins ensure that both you and your employee are held accountable to the plan. You'll want to touch base with the employee before a deadline, and again after the deadline date to make sure the goal was met.

Encourage your employee and work with him or her to ensure that the plan is helpful. If your employee is struggling to meet the goals of the plan, consider whether additional training might be useful. Ask for the employee's thoughts and ideas regarding the progress of the plan, or suggestions for improving it.

A performance action plan has a starting date and an ending date— it's not open-ended. If your employee needs more time to implement the plan and make the necessary improvements, consider whether that's realistic or a good idea. Whatever you do, stay in regular contact with the employee, and don't ignore the plan. If you do, your employee likely will simply forget about it, and you will have wasted your efforts.

Is It Working?

You'll easily know whether the plan is working by assessing the definable goals. If Joan is getting the bagels and rolls onto the shelves by 6 A.M., then she is following the terms of the performance action plan and the plan is working.

If the goals are not being met and the shelves are still empty at 6 A.M., the plan is not working. Or if Joan has fully stocked the shelves by 6 A.M., but she has neglected other aspects of her job to do so, the plan needs to be reviewed and changes made.

If the results on your plan are SMART—that is, specific, measurable, accountable, realistic, and timely—you should be able to tell with little trouble whether the plan is working. If you find that you can't gauge the results, you'll need to rework the plan.

Knowing When to Bail

Let's say that you identified an employee for whom a performance action plan seemed appropriate. After some consideration, you followed through with writing a plan, and you discussed the plan and its goals with your employee. After some discussion, and in response to her feedback and suggestions, you made some changes to the plan, and you and your employee agreed that it was workable.

Your employee said she was willing to work to complete the action plan, you both signed the plan, and you were feeling pretty optimistic that this employee could get back on track and fulfill the expectations of the job.

Two weeks into the plan, however, the plan clearly wasn't working. Worse yet, your employee either lost interest in the plan or had just been feigning interest from the start.

You discussed the problem with your employee, who agreed to work harder at implementing the terms of the plan. After another week, you could see that the employee still clearly had no interest in working toward the goals of the performance action plan—it wasn't going to work.

If this happens, you have to abandon the plan and move to the next step: beginning procedures to dismiss the employee. If the plan isn't working, and you've discussed the matter with the employee and given him or her another chance to move forward, then discard the plan.

You might find it necessary to bail on a performance action plan for other reasons as well:

- It becomes clear that the employee is incapable of following through to complete the goals stated on the plan.

- The employee simply is not a good fit for the job, and nothing is going to help him or her to be able to succeed in it. In that case, the employee should be reassigned or dismissed.

An unsuccessful performance action plan isn't the end of the world. If an employee is unwilling or unable to follow the terms of a plan that has been properly prepared and implemented, it's probably best to dismiss that employee.

The Least You Need to Know

- Performance action plans hold employees accountable for their actions and behaviors.
- Make sure the plan fits the circumstances.
- Involving employees in drawing up the plan gives them a sense of ownership and encourages buy-in.
- Follow through on the plan with regular check-ins and feedback.

Customer Feedback and Performance

In This Chapter

- Happy customers equal motivated employees
- Connecting employees with customers
- Remembering internal and external customers
- Using customer feedback in performance reviews

Customers are critical to any organization, whether it manufactures garage door springs, sells groceries, or provides spa services. Without customers, the plant, the grocery store, or the spa cannot remain viable.

Customers play another role that is often overlooked. Their feedback and interaction with employees can go a long way in boosting performance and getting—and keeping—workers invested in their jobs and organizations.

In this chapter, you'll learn how that happens, why it's so important, and how best to use customer involvement to keep your employees motivated and forward looking.

Why Everyone Needs Customer Contact and Feedback

In most workplaces, plenty of interaction takes place among employees, and adequate interaction also occurs between employees and managers. In many workplaces, interaction also occurs between employees, managers, and customers. In some cases, however, communication between customers and employees is scarce or even nonexistent, and that can result in significant performance problems.

Just as employees and managers require interaction, they also need interaction with customers—or, at least, feedback from customers. A direct correlation exists between customer satisfaction and employee performance.

Employees who get positive feedback from customers tend to be motivated and willing to work hard to make sure customers remain satisfied and happy. As employee performance improves, customers are increasingly satisfied, and employees become even more motivated, creating a win-win-win situation for employees, customers, and managers.

Without customer feedback and interaction, however, employees tend to lack the sense of excitement and satisfaction that accompanies knowing where they stand with customers. They don't know how they're doing, so they don't know whether improvement is necessary. They don't have a clear line of sight to the customer, and their goals and purpose become clouded and fuzzy. In short, they lose sight of why they're doing what they're doing.

When that happens, a job is just a job, not a piece of a bigger picture. Let's take a look at some other reasons employee contact and feedback are so important.

A Sense of Purpose

Just as employees need to know what you expect of them, they need to know what customers expect. Remember that the customer is at the center of the performance management program, which I discussed in Chapter 2. The four steps in that program—establish job performance standards and expectations, train, coach, and provide effective performance reviews—all revolve around your organization's internal and external customers.

If your employees don't understand the expectations of their customers, they can't effectively perform their jobs. Their efforts have to be linked to the needs and expectations of the customers, because that creates a sense of purpose.

If you instruct Tara to unpack six boxes of clothing that were delivered yesterday and get all the clothes either hung on hangers or folded and ready for display, chances are good that she'll perform those tasks. Chances are also good, however, that she won't be excited or motivated by the job; she'll simply go through the motions of getting it done. Why? Because the task isn't linked to a bigger picture. She's simply folding or hanging shirts and pants—she's not a part of any bigger goal.

If you tell her, however, that the reason she needs to unpack and prepare the clothing for display is that the store is starting its spring sale next week, and customers will expect the shelves to be fully stocked with attractive displays, her work suddenly has greater meaning. Now Tara is working to meet the expectations of customers instead of just hanging up shirts and folding pants. She's part of a bigger picture and is working toward the goal of getting ready for the spring sale. When customers arrive for the sale, Tara will have the satisfaction of knowing she was part of the team that prepared the store for them.

Job Enrichment

Job enrichment occurs when employees are allowed and encouraged to use the range of their abilities to take on more responsibility and tackle more interesting tasks. Job enrichment might mean that, in addition to unpacking the boxes and hanging and folding clothing, Tara gets to see the job through and actually create the display from which the clothing will be sold.

PERFORMANCE BOOST

The concept of job enrichment was first introduced in the late 1950s by Frederick Herzberg, a clinical psychologist and pioneer of management and motivational theory. Job enrichment, which is regarded as highly motivating to employees, involves creating challenge within a job, not just making the job bigger by adding more tasks.

Job enrichment entails task variety, task significance, and autonomy. When an employee is connected to customers through interaction and feedback, and when the job performed is linked to customers, those factors of job enrichment will be present. That means the employee will likely be far more motivated than he or she would be without the customer connection.

The Pride Factor

All employees want to be proud of the jobs they do and the organizations they work for. Customer feedback and interaction can go a long way toward creating and fostering a sense of pride, especially when it's shared with other employees.

An employee who experiences successful interaction with customers or receives positive feedback almost surely will experience a sense of pride. Within a workplace, pride is contagious and can be a powerful motivator among employees. Your customers can help promote pride among employees, but you need to facilitate sufficient interaction and opportunity for that to occur. When you notice a sense of pride among employees, do your best to cultivate it and keep it growing.

Remember that pride in the workplace begins at the top. If you're proud of your organization, your role within the organization, and your employees, your workers are likely to sense that pride and mirror it. A positive attitude tends to have a trickle-down effect, just as a negative one can, so don't be afraid to communicate and share your pride with employees.

The Big Picture

Contact with customers helps employees see the big picture and figure out how they, and the tasks they perform, fit into the organization's larger goals and mission. Contact with a customer may give employees a chance to see the product they've helped make being used, or to hear firsthand how a service they provided affected the customer.

> **CASE IN POINT**
>
> Michelle works for an agency that supplies assistance to people who need help with tasks of daily living. A client, Dave, hired the agency to help care for his elderly mother, Helen, who lived alone and had difficulty taking care of herself. Michelle assisted Helen for almost three years until Helen died. During that time, Michelle was dutiful about her job but didn't see the big picture. After Helen died, Michelle got a letter from Dave saying that her care had made it possible for Helen to remain in her own home, which had been important to her. Until Dave pointed this out, Michelle hadn't realized the impact of her work or how she fit into the bigger picture of the agency.

Lack of customer contact can be isolating for employees, most of whom are eager to know how their role within an organization affects the rest of the organization and contributes to its goals.

Customer contact and feedback is critical to employee motivation and performance. If your employees are isolated from customers, you must try to connect them.

How to Connect Employees with Customers

In some businesses, it's easy to connect employees and customers. In many instances, employee and customer contact is often necessary and unavoidable—think grocery stores, retail location, restaurants, health-care providers, and so forth. In some work settings, however, customers and employees don't have regular contact, or perhaps any contact at all.

An employee who works third shift in a manufacturing facility has little or no opportunity to interact with customers. The same goes for the overnight worker in the medical laboratory or the long-distance trucker who spends most of his time alone in his vehicle.

A good manager, however, will find a way to make employee–customer connections, even if those connections can't happen face to face.

Meet Customers at Workplace

If customers visit your workplace, you have the perfect opportunity to connect them with your employees, and you should take advantage of that. Even if employees work in a different part of the facility from where a customer is visiting, make a point to get them together.

When contact occurs, encourage employees to talk to customers and ask for feedback about the product or service they've provided. Find out if the customer is looking for anything to be done differently, and make sure employees introduce themselves.

If possible, introduce all the members of your team to customers, or at least those with whom customers may have contact.

Visit Customer Sites

If customers don't come to you, consider going to them—and taking employees with you. This doesn't have to be a full-fledged field trip, but taking an employee or two with you when you visit a customer can go a long way toward boosting performance by making employees feel that they are truly a part of the process and the larger good of the organization.

Of course, you'll want to let customers know if you're planning to take employees to a workplace, to make sure it's not a problem. Getting employees involved with customers on their turf is generally very effective and normally well received by both.

CASE IN POINT

One of my clients is a company that produces building materials. The boss recognized the importance of employee–customer interaction and also recognized that it wasn't happening at his workplace. The boss checked out which contractors working in the area of the company were using its building materials, selected 20 employees from both the production and office sides of the business, and went for a visit. Employees and contractors talked about product quality, delivery time, customer service, and other pertinent topics. The employees took the feedback they'd received back to their workplace and shared it with other employees. This resulted in noticeable improvements in quality, delivery time, and service. Everyone agreed that this linking of employees and customers was a great idea, and the visits continue.

Use Your Customer Service Department

Customer service representatives can be great sources of feedback regarding customers, because they are in frequent contact with them. These members of your organization should know what customers like, what they're not so crazy about, any particular problems a customer might be experiencing, and how customers perceive any members of your team with whom they might have contact.

One of my clients has the appropriate employees respond to customer complaints that he hears about from the customer service representatives. Customers are impressed when they get a call from the employee whose actions caused them to complain, and the employee feels good to be part of resolving the problem. It's a win-win situation.

Keeping in touch with customer service people can provide valuable information for you to share with your employees. If the information isn't confidential, ask to see customer service reports and logs to get a clear idea of what customers are saying. If there are complaints, address them with your employees and get their input on how to improve the situation, make customers happy, correct the action that spurred the complaint, and keep it from happening again.

Don't Forget Your Internal Customers

We normally think of customers in terms of those from outside of the organization, but internal customers are just as important. Internal customers are those within the company who are served by other employees. If the IT guy helps you with a computer problem, you're the internal customer. When you provide Ann with contact information for the location of the company's holiday party, Ann is the internal customer. If your boss asks you to provide him with a sales report, he's the internal customer. The new employee who asks you to show her how to use the copier is an internal customer.

Internal customers can also be other departments. The engineering department may feed ideas to the production department, or customer service may provide feedback to the shipping department.

CASE IN POINT

Jack is a manager at a medium-size design and manufacturing facility. His employees meet on a regular basis as internal customers to talk about how they're working together and what they need from each other. Their formula for communicating with each other is simple. The group that is providing a service to another group asks these questions:

- What do we do now that we should continue doing?
- What should we be doing more of?
- What should we be doing less of?
- What should we stop doing?
- Should we start doing anything?

This communication has improved production time, reduced the need for rework, reduced employee conflict, improved communication, and boosted employee performance.

Getting feedback from and maintaining contact with internal customers can help boost employee performance in the same way that external customers do. The feedback provides a sense of how employees are doing and areas where improvement might be necessary. This assures workers of their roles within the organization and keeps them motivated to help one another reach the company's goals.

Customer Surveys

Customer surveys can be excellent sources of information and should be conducted annually. Customers are normally willing to provide feedback when asked; just be sure not to overdo it and become an annoyance. The goal of a customer survey should be to learn two things:

- What do your customers think you're doing right?
- What changes would they like you to make?

Knowing what you're doing right allows you to continue to do it, and to use those strengths to attract other customers. Knowing what you're doing wrong allows you to improve your product or service to retain the customers you have and attract new ones.

Use customer surveys with new customers, customers you've had for a while, and former customers. Contacting former customers may be uncomfortable, but knowing why a customer left is invaluable. Additionally, sometimes customers leave over a misunderstanding that can be cleared up, and the customer can be brought back on board.

PERFORMANCE GAP

Jesse was an extremely enthusiastic new manager. He was determined to stay on top of every detail and do everything right. About six months after Jesse was hired, his boss started hearing rumblings from customers who were unhappy about his diligence in constantly seeking their input and asking for feedback. Customers said every interaction they had was followed up by a phone call or e-mail from Jesse, quizzing them on the service they'd received and asking for comments and suggestions. Customers had enjoyed and appreciated the attention at first, but it occurred too often; eventually, it became an intrusion. Customer surveys are great, but be sure they don't become a nuisance through overuse.

Customer surveys can be conducted by phone, although many companies have switched to online versions. Some companies offer incentives for customers to complete surveys, such as entering those who do for a drawing or giveaway.

Customer response cards handed out at the time of a sale or service are a popular means of surveying customers, and some companies hire and train "undercover" customers who evaluate service and report on their experiences.

When you've gathered and compiled information from a customer survey, you can share it with your employees and ask for their responses to the information. Remember to use positive responses to encourage employees, and use negative responses to make plans for improving the product or service provided.

Using Customer Feedback to Rate Employee Performance

Customer feedback should be ongoing, and you should keep track of the feedback affecting every member of your team. Customer feedback is an important tool you can use during employee reviews, which you'll learn all about in Chapter 15. Address feedback promptly once it's received; don't stash it away until review time. Use customer feedback as often as possible to motivate and encourage employees.

Most employees want to know how they're doing and will make improvements when necessary. Customer contact and feedback are important means of keeping team members involved and making them feel vested in the organization and ready to help the company meet its goals.

The Least You Need to Know

- Employee motivation and customer satisfaction are linked.
- Connecting customers and employees benefits both.
- Face-to-face contact is great, but other connections, such as customer surveys, are also useful.
- Customer feedback is a valuable employee performance review tool.

Performance and Reward

Many managers cringe at the thought of conducting performance reviews, but in Part 4, you'll learn that they're not a big deal for managers who have established clear expectations and kept a handle on how their employees are doing. Performance reviews are beneficial to both you and your employees and can result in better relationships. You'll also read about what motivates employees to higher performance levels—information that just might surprise you. And you'll learn how to use delegation to motivate your employees and grow your business.

The Performance Review Process

15

In This Chapter

- How performance reviews can benefit everyone
- Preparing for the performance review
- Involving employees in their reviews
- Building a plan for areas that need improvement
- Establishing new or continued expectations
- The importance of following up

Most people don't look forward to performance reviews, regardless of whether they're conducting the review or sitting on the receiving end of it. Still, performance reviews are generally recognized as necessary and important tools, and they are an integral part of the performance management cycle.

In this chapter, you'll get a clearer understanding of the importance of performance reviews and learn how to use them to your greatest advantage. You'll learn how to prepare for and conduct a review, and find out that performance reviews can actually serve as opportunities for strengthening your relationships with employees. In addition, you'll learn why reviews are such an important part of the performance management cycle and why the cycle can't work without them.

Why Every Boss Needs to Conduct Performance Reviews

I don't know how you feel about performance reviews, but if you're like most people (employees and managers alike), they're probably not at the top of your list of enjoyable activities. Employees often dread performance reviews because they don't know what to expect. Employees may anticipate that their managers will be judgmental or that the contents of the review won't be fair. They might be afraid that the review will affect their compensation, which can make it appear threatening and unpleasant. Managers, on the other hand, tend to dislike performance reviews because preparing for them takes time and conducting them can be an uncomfortable experience. Regardless of their positions, many people are reluctant to criticize or offer corrective feedback. It's a lot easier for most managers to either say nothing or give positive feedback than to discuss a shortcoming or problem, which is sometimes necessary during a performance review.

PERFORMANCE GAP

Employee performance assessments are more readily viewed as judgmental if an employee perceives the review to be personal. Stick to facts instead of focusing on personal behaviors. If an employee has been late four times in the past two months, for instance, simply present that fact. Don't refer to the tardiness as a bad habit of the employee or attach other personal traits to it.

Many employees and managers continue to dread performance reviews, but the fact remains that they are valuable and necessary tools for maintaining and boosting employee performance. Performance reviews are a necessary part of the performance management cycle, and even if you don't enjoy conducting them, they are part of your job as a manager.

When conducted properly, performance reviews can accomplish the following:

- **Facilitate a frank discussion of the employee's strengths and weaknesses.** Rarely is there time in a busy workplace for an in-depth conversation regarding an employee's performance. A scheduled performance review gives managers and employees an opportunity for frank discussion regarding both the employee's strengths and areas in which improvement might be necessary.

- **Allow time for discussion about other aspects of the job.** A performance review is a great time to discuss changing expectations, any shifts in company culture, and other matters that may not be dealt with on a regular basis. Smart managers understand that some of their best ideas come from employees when they are open to talking about ideas and listening to suggestions.

- **Offer a plan for improvement.** Instead of just addressing areas that need improvement, you and your employee can work together to plan how those improvements will occur.

- **Keep employees motivated for positive performance.** Recognition is a powerful motivator, and a performance review is a forum for recognizing all the good things your employee has accomplished. That doesn't mean you ignore everything else, but keep the motivation high by focusing on the positive.

PERFORMANCE BOOST

A recent Gallup poll revealed that 69 percent of workers questioned reported that receiving praise from an employer was more satisfying and motivating than money.

- **Maintain a positive manager–employee work relationship.** Performance reviews are great opportunities for coaching, and you and your employee have the ability to work as a team when planning for improvement or sustained performance levels. You'll share a goal of boosting employee performance, to benefit both the employee and the organization.

A performance review shouldn't be viewed as a final exam on which an employee's overall grade depends, although employees often tend to look at it as such. You might think of it instead as the last putt during a golf match. You wouldn't be there if you hadn't already completed all the other steps of the cycle or all the other shots that got you onto the green. And you can't complete the cycle—or the hole—without the last step, or the last putt. Everything before it brought you to that point, but the review, or the putt, is necessary to finish.

Each step of the performance management program discussed in Chapter 2—establish job performance standards and expectations, train, coach, and provide effective performance reviews—depends on the other three. For instance, you can't train an employee who doesn't understand the standards and expectations you've established. You can't be an effective coach to an employee who hasn't been trained.

A performance review gives you and the employee the opportunity to look at and discuss all the steps of the cycle and how well they worked—or didn't work. The performance review also enables you and your employee to set new goals and expectations for the coming year, which closes the performance management cycle and sets you up for it to begin again.

How to Prepare for a Performance Review

One of the reasons performance reviews get a bad rap is that often managers don't prepare for them properly. As a result, managers are uncomfortable as they stumble through the review, making the employee uncomfortable as well, and achieving much less than what they'd hoped.

PERFORMANCE GAP

Some companies have given up on performance reviews, declaring them to be overrated, counterproductive, or even useless. Others give up on them simply because managers don't want to take the time or make the effort to prepare. Regardless of the reason cited for doing so, giving up on performance reviews is a big mistake. You've read why reviews are important and the advantages they provide. Be willing to buy into them, and use some diligence in preparing for them.

In actuality, preparation for an employee performance review should be an ongoing and constant exercise. It's important to keep notes documenting your observations and interactions with your employees during the year. Those notes not only provide you with a record of employee performance, but they also serve as the basis of a performance review. Notes should include what you've observed, any discussion between you and the employee, the date of the interaction, and the context in which it occurred.

Another key in preparing for the review is to let your employees know in advance when the review will be held so that they also have time to prepare.

Assemble Data

As you refer to notes you've compiled throughout the year, remember to link them back to the employee's job description and established goals. After all, those notes and observances are based on whether the employee is meeting the standards and expectations that were stated.

In addition to your coaching notes, you'll want to have a copy of the goals and expectations that were established for the employee, a copy of the employee's job description, and a copy of the performance review form (see Chapter 3), which all employees should have seen when they first started the job and periodically since then. Remember that the review form is a valuable tool for reminding employees of what they're expected to be doing and what their performance evaluations will be based upon.

Any correspondence from others regarding the employee, such as a commendation or complaint from a customer, should also be included with your paperwork.

Review the data ahead of time to make sure you're familiar with all the information, and have copies made for the employee if you plan to review all the information with the employee or give it to him or her to look at after the review.

Decide What to Say

Employee performance evaluations are sometimes compared to job interviews. In both cases, it's best to have an idea of what you're going to say instead of making it up as you go along.

The point of the performance review is to discuss performance, so after a few pleasantries, limit your conversation to the matter at hand. Explain to the employee the purpose and benefits of the review, and the information on which the review is based.

PERFORMANCE BOOST

A performance review that has the status of a once-a-year major event takes on far more importance than it should have. When an employee has been trained and coached and monitored, with some less formal reviews thrown in throughout the year for good measure, he already has a good perspective on his job performance. In that case, the review won't likely contain any big surprises, because the employee and manager are already on the same page regarding job expectations and performance. Under those circumstances, the review isn't a dramatic event; it's just the last step of the performance management cycle.

Have the completed performance review form in front of you, and let the employee know what it is and the process used to complete it. You saw a sample form in Chapter 3, addressing employee performance such as knowledge of work, quality of work, work productivity, attendance and punctuality, follow-through, and how well the employee gets along with associates and customers.

If the employee is experiencing problems in any of those areas, or other areas included on the review form, you need to explain what you've observed. If the employee exceeded expectations in any area, make sure you acknowledge that as well.

Decide How to Say It

Hopefully, you and your employees have established an effective and comfortable means of communicating with one another, and that sort of communication will carry over to their performance reviews.

Reviews shouldn't be formal events; they should be opportunities for coaching and frank discussion. Your conversation should be professional, but don't think that you need to communicate differently than you normally do. You'll want to use a serious tone when discussing any problems, and don't be afraid to speak enthusiastically when talking about areas in which employees excel.

Anticipate Reactions and Questions

If you know your employees, you probably have some idea of how they will react to the contents of their performance reviews. If you anticipate that a particular employee might become defensive or upset during a performance review, be prepared for that. You might even want to have another manager on standby, in the event of a problem.

Generally, though, just be honest and willing to explain your assessment of the employee and answer any questions. An employee might want to know how you came up with the ratings you did, so be prepared to address that.

Preparation Checklist

Take a look at the following checklist and use it to help you prepare for a performance review. You can adapt and modify it as needed to make it work for you:

❏ Select a date and notify the employee.

❏ Select an appropriate location (think privacy).

❏ Advise the employee to be prepared to discuss the specifics of his or her performance, relative to the performance objectives established.

❏ Have the employee complete the appropriate portions of the performance review form.

❏ Review the established performance expectations for the employee.

❏ Review data from your previous monitoring of the employee.

❏ Determine the strengths and weaknesses of the employee's performance.

❏ Review your assessment with your supervisor to make sure you're in general agreement regarding the employee's performance.

❏ Make notes to assist you during the review. Be sure to include specific examples of performance to support your assessment.

❏ Plan an effective opening for the review, summarizing how it will proceed and the steps it will entail.

Involve Employees in Their Performance Reviews

An employee performance review shouldn't be one-sided, with you doing all the talking. It's important to get employees involved with their own reviews by having them express their opinions, rate themselves, and respond to your ratings. You can also use performance reviews as opportunities for employee career development.

Get Them to Rate Themselves

Before you even begin to discuss the ratings on your assessment form, ask your employee to tell you how things are going. Find out how the employee thinks he or she is doing. Demonstrate that you're interested by listening carefully, and encourage the employee to express his or her views at any point of the review.

PERFORMANCE GAP

Whatever you do, resist the temptation to rush through a performance review, even if it's your least favorite aspect of managing employees. Rushing can make employees feel like they're intruding on your time or that you're in a hurry to move on to something else. Block out about an hour for a review, and make sure the employee gets ample time to ask questions and express opinions.

If your opinion of the employee's performance is much different than his, be prepared to explain your rationale for how you've rated him. Ask the employee to be honest when rating himself; if you don't agree with how the employee rates him- or herself, ask for an explanation.

Encourage Them to Own Their Job Performances

Ideally, you and the employee being reviewed share a goal of improving the employee's performance. This ensures a positive working relationship and lets the employee know that you're behind him or her.

It's also important, however, for the employee to take responsibility for individual performance, regardless of its level. Your employee should be interested in and willing to talk about his or her job performance, whether or not it meets expectations. If the employee is experiencing problems, encourage him or her to talk about what's going on, and ask why he or she thinks the problems are occurring. If the employee is meeting or exceeding expectations, he or she should be able to explain how that's happening.

The job performance belongs to the employee, so the employee needs to be aware of how he or she is performing and understand how it affects him or her, the rest of the team, and the organization.

Provide Opportunity for Career Development

Be sure to leave some time during the review for the employee to talk about his hopes for the future within the company. A performance review can provide excellent opportunity for a frank discussion on where the employee might be headed.

Norris was a good worker and well regarded by his co-workers and manager, Maria. He had mentioned once or twice to Maria that he was interested in advancement, but they didn't have a chance to discuss that possibility in any depth until Norris's performance review.

Norris and Maria had a chance during the review to talk about Norris's aspirations and for Maria to share her thoughts about possible opportunities for him. By the end of the review, they'd decided that Norris should apply for a production supervisor job the next time one was available, and that Maria would recommend Norris for participation in an emerging leaders training program for high-potential employees.

The performance review gave Norris a chance to describe his aspirations, and Maria was able to act on them. Together they were able to work out a plan to move the employee ahead. If the employee has been performing at a less-than-adequate level, you can work out a plan to get that person back on track.

Reinforce the Positive with Specific Examples

If you've kept good coaching notes, you should be able to provide your employees with specific examples of positive job performance. Using specific examples is far more effective than speaking in general terms, and your employees will appreciate that you've paid attention to what they've been doing. Reinforcing positive performance goes a long way toward sustaining morale and keeping employees motivated.

Build a Plan for Improvement

If improvement is necessary in any area, work with your employee to plan for how it will occur. Your employee may well realize that there is a performance problem and will be grateful for a plan to fix it.

CASE IN POINT

Leon had been promoted to receiving supervisor about two months before his performance review, and the job wasn't going as he and his manager had expected. Significant performance gaps had caused some problems for the company, and Leon's manager wasn't sure how to resolve the situation. During the performance review, Leon said he understood that he was having difficulties in the job, but he didn't want to admit it because he thought he'd be replaced. Together, Leon and his manager came up with a doable plan for improvement, and Leon was able to begin working toward the goals of the plan. Soon he was not only meeting expectations, but exceeding them.

After identifying performance areas that require improvement, and citing specific examples of performance gaps, let your employee take the lead in coming up with a plan for improvement. This allows the employee to acknowledge the problem and take ownership of correcting it. Set specific and measurable goals, such as "By two weeks from today, all the reports from last year will be recorded and filed, and by four weeks from today, all the reports received this year will be recorded and filed."

Your role is to work with employees to assess their abilities to make changes, and to help them come up with realistic goals. If you know it's going to take far longer than two weeks to finish filing last year's reports, don't let an employee set him- or herself up to fail by setting unrealistic goals.

After establishing a plan for improvement, make sure the employee understands it by having him or her confirm the conversation you've had. Then get the plan in writing for both of you to sign.

Using the Review to Establish New or Continued Expectations

The performance review is a great opportunity to establish new expectations for an employee. It affords an opportunity for frank discussion about the employee's work, as well as a chance to set up the employee for the next year.

If the employee will be facing a change in job responsibilities or tasks, you'll certainly want to discuss the expectations associated with that. If improvement is necessary in some areas, it's necessary to establish or re-establish clear expectations for how the change will occur.

If change is occurring with the department or organization, new expectations will need to be established to address that. If the employee is doing well and will be continuing in the same position, you may simply have to confirm the existing expectations and establish an agreement that the employee will continue to meet or exceed them.

Following Up After the Review

A performance review loses its value if it lacks follow-up. You can be completely prepared, conduct the best review in the world, and come up with a great plan for improvement, but if there's no follow-up, it's a pretty good bet that nothing will change.

After the review, you should prepare a summary that states your overall evaluation and the major aspects of observed behavior that support that evaluation. Review the summary with the employee you've evaluated, get that person's signature along with yours, and send the form to human resources or the appropriate person. You and the employee should each get a copy of the summary to keep on file.

A manager should constantly be monitoring performance, but it's particularly important after a performance review if you've established a plan for improvement. Tell your employee that you'll be following up, and then check in on a regular basis to determine whether the plan is on track.

Check for Increased Effort

At the very least, you should expect increased effort from an employee whose performance has been problematic. After you and the employee have acknowledged the problem and created a plan for improvement, you should expect an immediate and noticeable effort from the employee.

If you don't see it, you'll need to address the matter with the employee. A lack of effort from an employee who has agreed to work to improve performance doesn't speak well to commitment or attitude. Don't wait to address the matter, because the employee could interpret your silence as a sign that you aren't serious about keeping the improvement plan on track, or that you aren't following up on the review.

Check for Improved Performance

When it's clear the employee is making an effort to improve performance, use the measurable goals you both have established to determine whether there really is improvement.

If the employee is trying and performance is improving, the performance review likely has served its purpose and the employee will soon be meeting expectations. If no improvement has occurred, you'll need to readdress the issue. Look at whether the goals you set are realistic. Ask the employee if something is preventing him or her from boosting performance, and ask what you might be able to do to help.

If the employee is making a real effort and simply is unable to improve her performance to meet expectations, the expectations may be unrealistic for that employee.

Get a Second Opinion

Just as it's a good idea to get a second opinion about an employee's performance before the review, checking in with your supervisor after the review can help you be sure you and the employee are staying on track.

It's particularly helpful to get a second opinion if the plan for improvement that you and the employee drew up isn't working, or if the employee doesn't seem to be making an effort to boost performance.

Managers sometimes have trouble remaining objective concerning employee performance. It's easy to get frustrated with someone who doesn't appear to care about improving performance. On the flip side, you may be sympathetic to an employee experiencing performance difficulty because you know something about a personal situation that's affecting his or her work, and you're unwilling to take firm action to correct the problem. Your supervisor may give you some needed perspective.

The Least You Need to Know

- Performance reviews are notoriously unpopular, but they're generally considered useful and important.
- Good preparation is essential to a successful review.
- Employees should be actively involved in the review process.
- Use the review to establish new expectations or come up with a plan for improvement, when necessary.

Development Plans

In This Chapter

- Why development plans are important
- What to include in a plan
- Helping employees plan for advancement
- Keeping the plan moving forward

It's always a pleasure to manage an employee whom you know has what it takes to move to the next level within the job or the organization, particularly when you know that the employee is eager to do just that.

Shepherding an employee up the ladder requires a great deal of coaching, mentoring, and direction from you. At the same time, you need to be planning for someone to take that person's place and keep things running smoothly as he or she makes the transition to another position.

It's a rewarding process, though, and one that every manager should aspire to. In addition to coaching and mentoring, you can use a development plan to help your employee advance. In this chapter, you'll learn what a development plan is and how to make sure it serves the intended purposes of moving an employee forward.

What Is a Development Plan?

A development plan is a tool that you, a manager, can use to motivate staff members and help further their goals within your organization. Development plans generally are put into place for motivated employees who are looking to move ahead, to take the next step. These include the front-desk receptionist who is looking to move into an office manager position, the licensed practical nurse who aspires to become a nurse practitioner, the salesperson who hopes to double the number of district sales, and the caseworker striving to become a casework manager.

Development plans identify an employee's goals and list the steps necessary to achieve them. They are useful for moving employees ahead because they concentrate on the individual's strengths and skills, as well as the steps necessary to move up the ladder. Most employees respond positively to the use of development plans because they are intended to advance the individual's goals.

Some organizations, including the U.S. government, encourage employees to initiate development plans for themselves as they contemplate future job opportunities. Other organizations hand-pick employees for whom they feel development plans are applicable and motivating. Other companies don't use them at all.

> **PERFORMANCE BOOST**
>
> Development plans are nearly the opposite of performance action plans (see Chapter 13), which point out performance gaps and take measures to fix them. Development plans are a lot more fun for managers because they target employees who already are performing well and help move them to the next level.

Some managers argue that development plans, often referred to as individual development plans, are ineffective because they tend to focus on employee weaknesses and simply recommend training to strengthen those areas. Critics argue that employees can't be great at every aspect of their jobs, and no amount of training will enable them to master the areas in which they fall short.

The purpose of a development plan, however, should be to focus on an employee's strengths and figure out how you and the employee can work together to channel those strengths toward opportunities for advancement. Plans can be short term or long term, depending on an employee's goals. An employee may use a series of development plans to establish and reach long-term goals.

Where Is Your Employee Going?

The first thing a development plan should address is the aspirations of the employee. Is Amy looking to advance from a bookkeeping to an accounting position? Jon from assistant manager to department manager? Freddie from art director to creative director?

You can help employees establish realistic and doable goals by explaining the hierarchy of the organization if they don't fully understand it, helping them learn the qualifications for the desired job, and making sure the goals they set meet the needs of the company. If the organization is already management heavy, for example, it may not be looking for additional managers in the next six months. On the other hand, if a department is going to be enlarged and given greater responsibility, there may well be job opportunities there.

PERFORMANCE BOOST

Sometimes managers observe potential in an employee and initiate development plans to help that employee climb the ladder. Other times employees initiate development plans, often without putting any name to them. An employee might say something like, "You know, I think I could be really effective as a manager in this company. How would I look into making that happen?" At that point, you can steer the employee toward a development plan, if applicable.

Make sure an employee's goals are set within the current framework of the company. If the organization will be downsizing, for instance, it could affect an employee's short-term goals. Likewise, goals might have to be altered if the company announces plans to expand operations and hire new staff. You can assist by seeing which direction the organization is heading and what it might require from staff in the coming months and years.

Help employees to look at both short- and long-term goals as they consider their place within the organization. A development plan can address long-term goals while identifying short-term goals that actually serve as milestones toward reaching those longer goals.

And remember to make sure the goals set are SMART: specific, measurable, accountable, realistic, and timely. If you'd like to review those categories, flip back to Chapter 2.

What's the Plan for Getting There?

Once an employee has identified a goal, you'll want to help determine the steps necessary to get there. Will additional training be required? If so, how will it be facilitated? Will the employee need to take more classes or go back to school?

Many companies are making do with fewer employees these days and expecting more of those employees. Will your employee be able to continue to meet the expectations of the job while working to advance his or her position? Encourage the employee to be honest in an assessment and to note any anticipated stumbling blocks.

 PERFORMANCE GAP

Respect the limitations of a manager-employee relationship while mentoring an employee. You can offer work-related suggestions and insights, but stay away from an employee's personal life. Even if you think that Wendy, a single mom with a bunch of kids, is crazy for signing up for night classes she'll need to earn a degree, it's not up to you to express that.

Advise your employee that the plan must be realistic to work. Maintaining the schedule and workload comes before taking on a new commitment to enroll in classes three nights a week at a location an hour away from her house. Will an employee really be able to finish nursing courses in three years, in light of her many other responsibilities, or should classes be spread out over three and a half or four years? You'll need to employ strong coaching and mentoring skills, while being careful not to overstep boundaries.

Once your employee, with your help, has identified applicable training and development opportunities to move toward personal goals and has had the training approved, it's up to the employee to make sure it happens. He or she should take responsibility, with you as the overseer, for making sure someone can take over the necessary parts of the job during training, that registration is confirmed, that payment has been authorized, and so forth.

CASE IN POINT

Jess had been working in the coffee shop near her home since she was 16 years old, and she eventually took over the responsibilities of managing it. Leda, the owner of the business, increasingly depended on Jess as she spent less time at the shop. When Leda decided to retire, Jess expressed interest in buying the business. She knew the coffee business well but had no formal training or education in owning a business. Leda and Jess crafted a development plan that included Jess earning an associate's degree and other milestones. Leda also agreed to delay her retirement for six months to allow Jess time to meet her goals. Jess is now the owner and manager of a successful coffee shop.

If your organization isn't in a financial position to offer extensive or expensive training or development for an employee who's eager to move ahead, help your employee come up with ideas for other means of learning the job. Perhaps this could be job-shadowing an employee who holds the position now, or assisting with a project in the targeted department. As you read in Chapter 12, many types of training are available, including the following:

- Online distance learning
- Exposure to supervisory duties
- Work on a project team
- Seminars or webinars
- Workshops
- Job rotation

If time and money for training are in short supply within your organization, you might have to be an advocate for an employee who's looking to move up the ladder. Think about how you might help your employee present the case to others who can influence whether he or she has an opportunity for advancement.

When you and the employee have a plan in place, you both should sign and date it. This isn't to make the plan a binding or formal document, but to acknowledge that you both understand how the employee plans to move forward.

Who's Qualified to Take His or Her Place?

Employees working toward advancement within the organization will earn the respect of management if they express concern over who will take their place as they move forward and how their current job can continue to progress smoothly. These concerns portray a team player who's concerned about the good of the organization, not just personal career advancement.

You can help your employees by making sure their job descriptions are current. Chances are, capable workers obtained some additional responsibilities in the past months or years that should be reflected in the job description.

Review job performance standards and expectations, and talk with employees about any concerns they might have about the current job. Maybe some aspects of a job didn't run as smoothly as possible, and an employee may have ideas for streamlining the job or making it more productive. Ask for ideas concerning who might replace an employee in the current position, and develop some ideas together for training the replacement worker. What kind of training does the current employee think would help? What areas of the job might require additional training time? Other questions might include the following:

- Can you think of procedures that might be put in place to make the job operate more smoothly?

- What are the most difficult parts of this job?

- Can some areas of the job be delegated to an assistant?

- What personal qualities do you feel contribute to being successful in this job?

- Would you have welcomed additional responsibility in this position?

- How did this position prepare you to deal with customers/ co-workers/management?

- How do other workers within the department perceive this job?

- Do you feel that you received appropriate supervision?

- Did you fully understand the performance expectations of this job?

Regard this time with your employee as a chance to brainstorm and obtain information that will be useful for you and the person who will replace him or her.

Following Up on Development Plans

Development plans are like any other type of plan. You can work hard to set up and produce a great document, but it's meaningless if you and your employee don't follow up on it. If that happens, the plan becomes just a meaningless exercise and a significant waste of time.

Remember that development plans are not cast in stone, but are likely to change as time passes. A particular training that you thought would be available might become unavailable, or an opportunity you didn't know about might present itself.

The employee's plans also might change, so the move you'd been working toward no longer makes sense. Changes within the organization could send your plans awry, too. Even as the plan changes—or perhaps especially as it changes—you'll need to keep in contact with the employee and encourage him or her to keep the plan moving forward.

PERFORMANCE GAP

If you agree to work with an employee who's eager to advance and offer help with a development plan, serious trust issues can arise if you don't follow up on your offer. You and the employee will invest significant time and effort in the employee's future plans; not following through sends a message to your employee that you don't care enough to see the effort through to completion.

How to Keep a Plan on Track

Plan to meet with your employee quarterly to assess the development plan. As the manager, you should be checking in and talking with your employee regularly, so you'll be aware of how the plan is progressing between those meetings. Quarterly sit-downs, however, will enable you and your employee to really talk about progress, discuss any issues or problems, and make sure your employee is getting time for additional training or whatever is necessary to continue on track. You'll also be able to see whether changes to the plan are necessary or adjustments need to be made.

How to Evaluate Progress

Evaluating the progress of your employee's development plan doesn't need to be a formal process, but it's important that you stay informed. It's a good idea to have your employee report to you after completing training or accomplishing another of the goals in the plan, especially if you're not due for your quarterly meeting.

Use the goals of the plan as established milestones, and keep track of which have been completed. Your employee could use a chart or electronic tracking program, or simply write brief summaries of what's been completed.

As long as you and your employee remain in contact so you're both aware of how the plan is proceeding, the method you choose to evaluate the progress of the plan isn't overly important. The important point is for the employee to continue working toward the goals and keeping track of what has been achieved.

Keeping Yourself and Your Employees Accountable

Upwardly mobile employees (and managers) tend to be busy employees. They're generally willing to go above and beyond in their job responsibilities, and they're willing to help out whenever necessary. For those and other reasons, goals put forth in a development plan sometimes get pushed to the background or even forgotten. Quarterly meetings keep your employees accountable for meeting their goals, as do your frequent check-ins. Establish a frequency with which you want employees to update you on their progress, and hold them accountable to meeting those time frames.

PERFORMANCE BOOST

Some managers reward employees as they achieve the goals of the plan, even if it's just with a candy bar or movie tickets.

It's a good idea to set deadlines for meeting goals, with the understanding that they, too, may be subject to change, due to circumstances beyond the control of you and your employees. Advise your employees to try to remain as structured as possible within their plans, to keep them moving, and to keep track of their progress, as discussed earlier.

Development plans are primarily the responsibilities of the employees who are using them. Your job, as the manager, is to assist them, encourage them to be accountable for meeting the goals they've set, and check in with them frequently to keep the plans viable.

A Sample Development Plan

The following plan demonstrates that development plans don't have to be complicated or fancy. They merely need to state objectives, a plan for meeting objectives, possible contingencies, and a plan for follow-up.

Employee Development Plan

Employee Name: Ron Wilson

Job Title: Senior Manufacturing Engineer

Department: Manufacturing & Engineering

Manager Name: Rich Andrews

Manager Title: Manager of Manufacturing Engineering

Employee's Current Performance

Ron is doing an outstanding job in his current role. He is dedicated, knowledgeable, and responsive to the needs of the manufacturing department. Ron has expressed interest in the newly created position of supervisor of manufacturing engineering, but he lacks supervisory skills and experience.

Expected Performance

Because Ron is a valued employee, his manager supports his desire to seek additional responsibility. With this in mind, his manager has developed a fast-track schedule of learning and work responsibilities designed to prepare Ron for consideration as the new supervisor.

Development Goals

Ron will need to learn how to supervise co-workers and projects. He will also need to develop the performance management skills (setting expectations, coaching, and reviewing performance) required of supervisors in our company.

Development Plan

- Ron will complete the four-day supervisory skills training course on the next available date.

- Upon completing the training, Ron will be put in charge of a project designed to help test his leadership skills. This will involve designing the process for the new series of flow valves. He will be asked to serve as team leader for this project.

- Ron will also begin to attend the biweekly staff meeting with his manager for exposure to the "big picture" of the company.

Follow-Up Plans

In three months, Rich and Ron will meet for a formal review to evaluate the success of the plans. At that time, they will decide what further training steps are required. If the review is favorable and no further training is required, Ron will formally be offered the position of supervisor of manufacturing engineering.

Employee's Signature _____   Date _____

Manager's Signature _____   Date _____

The Least You Need to Know

- Development plans can help develop employees' skills and advance their careers within the company.
- Plans can be initiated by you or by your employee.
- Plans include summary of performance, goals, and a plan to achieve those goals.
- Deliberate follow-up is important to keep development plans on track.

Pay and Performance

In This Chapter

- Linking pay to the three parts of performance
- Determining pay or pay ranges
- Explaining salaries to employees
- Why base pay is not the total compensation picture

No question about it, pay is important—but it's by no means the only thing that motivates employees. Knowing that, however, doesn't mean you won't have to sometimes grapple with issues concerning compensation, which can be one of the most controversial topics of the workplace. Compensation is important to leadership because it's one of the biggest expenses of the company. It's important to employees, too, not just because money is necessary for survival, but because it's seen as a measure of fairness or unfairness and an indication of their value to the company. A lot of emotion is wrapped up in compensation.

In this chapter, you'll learn how to navigate the sometimes thorny field of employee pay and you'll see how compensation can be a great means of paying for performance.

The Relationship Between Pay and Performance

In an ideal workplace, the best employees—those who contribute the most toward the goals and mission of the company—would get the most pay. As you know, that's not always the case.

So what is the relationship between pay and performance? Or, at least, what should it be? First, let's understand what performance is based upon.

Performance involves three parts:

- Job accountability
- Goal attainment
- Value-added qualities

Job accountability simply means whether an employee meets the requirements of the job description. Does he achieve the defined responsibilities of the job?

If Nathan's job description states that he is to attain new customers by following up on all requests for information, website queries, trade show attendance, leads from direct mailings, and tips from others within the organization, the question is whether he performs those tasks on a regular basis. Meeting the responsibilities of the job should be the first area of performance considered.

> **PERFORMANCE BOOST**
>
> The best time to link performance to pay is during the first step of the performance management cycle, when you're establishing job performance standards and expectations. If your organization uses a bonus system, explain to employees how it ties in with how well they meet the responsibilities of their job description and attain their goals. Re-establish those links during job performance evaluations.

The second area, goal attainment, involves whether employees meet the goals they've set for themselves. Has Nathan followed up on all website queries within 24 hours of posting? Has he called on the four potential customers he met at the trade show? Those goals are established, not arbitrary, and are important in measuring performance.

The third factor, value-added qualities of performance, is harder to measure but no less important. These are qualities such as showing up on time to appointments, being able to communicate effectively with customers and co-workers, coming up with and sharing ideas for improvement, maintaining a positive attitude, and being willing to stay late to finish a timely task.

Pay should be based on these three areas of performance. It's your job, then, as a manager, to ensure that this happens, as much as you're able.

How Do You Know How Much to Pay Someone?

This age-old question is an enduring problem for managers and is the source of much discussion, debate, and sometimes conflict. That's because, as you read earlier, employee compensation involves a lot of emotion.

Jackie is distraught because Cho makes more money than she does, but Cho never, ever stays after 5:30 and Jackie is often at her desk until 6:30 or later.

Brandon didn't get a raise after his last performance review. He understands that the company is doing everything it can to reduce spending during a difficult economic climate, but he's still upset because he knows of two people who did get raises and he feels that he's being taken advantage of.

For these employees, their salaries are tied into how they perceive they're valued by the company and a sense of what's fair. Likely Jackie would be fine with earning $20 an hour if she didn't know that Cho was earning $22. Brandon might be okay with no raise if nobody else had gotten one.

As a manager, you may determine, or help to determine, how much an employee gets paid. If so, you'll probably work within a salary range and recommend where your employees should fall within that range.

Your recommendation should be based upon the employee's performance, comprised of the three areas described in the previous section. Pay is also based on factors over which you have no control, such as geography, the type of business you're in, prior experience of the employee, salary levels set within the company, the current job market and availability of employees, and others.

Work within the guidelines for pay set by your organization, remember to keep salary in alignment with the goals and mission of the organization, and ensure consistency between performance and compensation. Once pay has been determined, it's your job to make sure employees know how it was determined and why.

PERFORMANCE GAP

Don't be tempted to use different standards for different employees when determining compensation. Nothing outrages workers more than knowing, or even perceiving, that they've been treated unfairly. All employees must be held to the same standard so that they know they've been treated fairly when it comes to pay. At all costs, avoid the slightest perception that pay is influenced by a person's gender, race, religion, sexual preference, or national origin—all of which are illegal.

Make Sure Employees Understand Why They Earn What They Do

Many managers dread having to talk to employees about their pay because the discussion can be uncomfortable, emotional, or even confrontational. The best thing you can do to defuse a conversation about pay is make sure the employee understands that pay is based on performance, know how performance was evaluated, and understand why the employee is paid that amount.

Explain the company's compensation system and the salary range for the employee's particular position. Explain that salary is based on factors such as the responsibilities the position entails and how well the employee has achieved personal goals.

If the employee's pay was influenced by company performance or the general state of the economy, explain that as well. Point out what the employee needs to accomplish to rise to the next level of performance and achieve a salary increase, and remind the employee that he or she also may be eligible for nonmonetary rewards, such as special assignments, increased recognition, or added flexibility to working hours.

If the employee is receiving company benefits, be sure to explain that benefits and payroll taxes are also part of the total compensation. The more educated your employees are regarding their salaries and the company's payroll policies, the less likely they'll be dissatisfied and spark morale problems or increased employee turnover.

How Important Is Pay to Employees?

Of course, a paycheck is a good thing. But it's not the only motivating factor for employees. Other factors include these:

- Job challenge
- Career opportunities
- Interesting work
- Flexible work schedule
- A supportive workplace
- Recognition of achievement
- Opportunity to work as part of a team
- Investment in the goals of the company
- Fairness in the workplace
- Good communication
- Feeling of being appreciated
- Sense of camaraderie

Even if all factors are in place, however, employees still expect, and rightly so, to be appropriately and fairly compensated. When the country, and much of the rest of the world, went into recession near the end of 2007, many workers were forced to forego salary increases or take pay cuts to keep their jobs. You can bet that none of those workers were happy, but most probably understood that the actions were necessary to keep the organization viable.

Generally, however, employees expect to receive compensation that's comparable to that of employees in other, similar jobs and companies. As a manager, you can help employees understand how they're compensated by explaining all of the employer's costs for their compensation.

PERFORMANCE BOOST

As much as you would like for your employees to never discuss their pay with one another, you know that such conversations occur. And although you can make it known that talking about salary is highly discouraged, there's no way to legally enforce such a policy. Under the National Labor Relations Act, it is not legal for an employer to prohibit discussion about wages and salary.

Base Pay

Base pay, also called base wages, is the money an employee earns for performing the duties described in the job description and meeting the established performance standards. It's the basic salary. Base pay is established at the time the job begins, and it changes over the course of the job based on factors such as added responsibilities, promotions, demotions, number of hours worked, job location, and so forth.

Base pay can be hourly or salaried. The wages of a hourly worker can vary, depending on the number of hours worked within a particular pay period. Also, hourly workers might earn a higher pay if the work is performed on a weekend or holiday, or if they've worked more than the number of hours agreed to for a particular pay period.

Salaried workers receive the same amount of money for each pay period, regardless of the number of hours worked.

Some organizations, particularly government agencies and the U.S. military, use base pay charts to establish a pay structure for the entire organization. The structured pay applies to all workers at various levels of the organization. Base pay can also depend on wage standards, such as minimum wage requirements. The federal minimum wage was established in 1938 as an effort to prevent sweat shop labor, and was increased to $7.25 in July 2009. Except in a few cases, states are required to pay workers at least as much as the federal minimum wage. Washington has the highest minimum wage of any state, set at $8.55.

Benefits

Job benefits have become increasingly important in the last decade or so, with increasing influence on whether workers accept jobs, stay in them, or move to other jobs. It's not unusual to talk to an employee who took a job for no other reason than that it provides good, or even acceptable, benefits. For example, Karen's husband lost his job and has been unemployed for more than a year. She works as a cook in an assisted care facility, even though, with a bachelor's degree in business and a master's degree in psychology, she's overqualified for the job, which requires only a high school or equivalency degree. Why? She needs benefits for herself and her husband.

Nancy, whose husband is self-employed, is a sales representative in a job that requires her to be on the road constantly, visiting convenience stores and other locations in which the company places its product. Why? She needs benefits for herself, her husband, and their three kids.

Benefits, sometimes called fringe benefits, include insurance, such as health, life, and disability; paid leave, such as vacation, sick days, and personal days; supplemental pay for shift differentials, overtime, and other factors; retirement or savings plans, such as pensions or 401(k)s; and legally required benefits, such as Social Security, Medicare, unemployment insurance, and worker's compensation.

Some jobs offer great benefits to employees and their families, and certain benefits are required by law for employees who work a certain number of hours and meet other requirements. Other jobs provide few or no benefits. Many part-time workers get no benefits, meaning that someone who works several part-time jobs might work more hours than a full-time worker but not receive any benefits.

CASE IN POINT

Employees of the search engine giant Google get an astounding array of benefits—way beyond comprehensive health care, vision, and dental plans; 401(k)s; and 15 vacation days after one year. Employees can also take advantage of free lunch and dinner, an on-site doctor, shuttle service to and from work, child care, tuition reimbursement, and financial planning services.

The company pays for any benefits provided, and these should be counted as part of an employee's total compensation.

According to numbers released by the Bureau of Labor Statistics, the average compensation of a civilian employee, which includes state and local government and private industry workers, was $29.40 per hour in September 2009.

The makeup of that total compensation is as follows:

- Wages and salaries: $20.50 per hour

- Insurance benefits: $2.53 per hour

- Paid leave: $2.04 per hour

- Supplemental pay: 76¢ per hour

- Retirement and savings: $1.29 per hour

- Legally required benefits: $2.28 per hour

If you add up those numbers, you'll find that wages and salaries account for nearly 70 percent of total compensation, with benefits combining for about 30 percent. Remember, that's an average, but it gives you an idea of how benefits increase the cost of total compensation. Your employees should be aware of the total value of their compensation, not just its base pay portion.

Benefits normally are not linked to performance because they are extended to everyone within the organization who meets certain standards, such as having been employed for 90 days or working at least 30 hours a week. However, they are an important and significant part of compensation.

Bonuses

While benefits usually aren't linked to performance, they should be directly connected. In fact, it's generally agreed that bonuses that aren't linked to employee performance should be scrapped entirely. Bonuses linked to companywide performance can also be valuable, because they invest employees in the success of the business and link individual performance with that of the overall operation.

Bonuses that are handed out in a seemingly random or arbitrary manner can end up causing resentment among employees. Some companies hand out year-end bonuses, and if they're based on the performance level of each employee, that's okay. To simply hand out a bonus because it's the end of the year and employees expect them, however, can be a dangerous practice.

CASE IN POINT

One of my clients, a company that serves the aerospace industry, instituted an innovative form of bonus system that it calls "spot awards." Anyone at any level within the company can nominate a colleague for doing something outstanding. It can be great customer service, a safety innovation, a cost-saving measure—anything that exceeds expectations. The nominator fills out a form that is given to management. The nominee receives a certificate and an extra $25 in his paycheck. In addition, management reviews all of the nominations every quarter and selects an overall winner, who gets an additional $300 in his check. Employees and management are 100 percent behind this program and say it keeps staff members motivated and excited to exceed their job responsibilities.

What happens when the economy is in a downturn and the company is cutting expenses in any manner possible, including year-end bonuses? Workers who have come to expect and count on these bonuses will likely be upset when they don't get them. That can cause disruptions and not motivate employees.

Bonuses that are directly linked to performance, however, can motivate workers and boost performance.

Some examples in which an organization might reward employees with bonuses include the following:

- Salespeople exceed their quotas.

- Employees come up with ideas for saving money or increasing productivity.

- Workers bring new customers to the company.

- Accounts receivable workers exceed expectations for collections.

- Workers finish projects ahead of schedule or come in under budget on projects.

- Employees put in more hours than expected.

- Team members have excellent attendance records.

These kinds of bonuses are linked directly to performance, and they create incentive for employees to boost performance in order to earn them. They're good for both the employees and the organization: employees receive extra compensation, and the organization benefits from the employees' work.

PERFORMANCE BOOST

If your company currently hands out year-end or other types of bonuses not linked to employee performance, consider ending them. If you feel that you can't pull the plug for employees who already receive the bonuses, tell them that the bonus money they expect will be divided and included in their paychecks over the course of the year. That way, those employees don't feel that they've lost anything, and you don't have to give year-end bonuses to any new employees.

If you plan to use bonuses to boost employee performance, be sure that employees understand the standards used to determine who will get them. For instance, you might tell your sales employees that anyone who exceeds the monthly quota will get $100, and those who exceed it for three months in a row will get a $500 bonus.

Decide ahead of time how much bonus money you'll have available, and don't allocate so much to bonuses that it affects other areas of the organization.

Bonuses can be great means of motivating employees, but if you're rewarding productivity, be careful that the product or service doesn't suffer because of an employee who's working toward the bonus and not paying attention to quality. You'll need to establish guidelines regarding bonuses and make sure that they apply across the board, to let employees know they're being treated fairly.

The Least You Need to Know

- Establish a clear relationship between pay and performance.
- Make sure you understand your organization's salary structure.
- Communicate the salary structure to employees.
- Compensation includes more than base pay.
- Use bonuses wisely to motivate employees and boost performance.

Nonmonetary Rewards

In This Chapter

- Seeing the value of nonmonetary rewards
- Setting up the criteria
- Offering nonmonetary rewards that make sense
- Using recognition as a reward
- Matching the reward to the employee
- Figuring out whether your rewards program is working

You know that you've got to pay your employees to perform, or even to show up to work. And you understand how monetary pay is used to reward employees who perform at least as well as they're expected to. What about nonmonetary rewards? Will an employee really be motivated to perform better by the promise of a gift certificate to his favorite restaurant or a couple of tickets to a hockey game? The answer is, yes, if the rewards are given correctly.

In this chapter, you'll learn that nonmonetary rewards can be valuable tools for boosting employee performance, but they need to make sense to employees and be in line with the goals of your company.

Why Nonmonetary Rewards Are Valuable

When the process is thought out and the rewards are appropriate, nonmonetary rewards are valuable because they increase recognition for employees who have performed well. They offer something above and beyond the paycheck.

Most employees feel like they've earned their paychecks and they deserve the pay. They expect, and rightly so, to be compensated for doing the work they agreed to. Nonmonetary rewards, however, go above and beyond the paycheck. They single out valuable employees and let them know they're appreciated and valued. Survey after survey has shown that, more than anything, most employees want their work to be recognized and appreciated. Bosses who are unable or unwilling to buy into that finding will never get the best from their employees.

In some ways, teams of employees aren't all that much different from baseball or football teams. The members want to be part of the team and want their team to win, but they also would like to have a little individual recognition and attention for themselves. It's great to have your team win the game, but it's even sweeter if you hit the home run that brings in three runners and clinches the title, or if you're named the most valuable player in the playoff game.

 PERFORMANCE GAP

Some managers don't like rewards of any sort. They feel that a paycheck is enough reward for showing up and working a job. Why would you give an employee anything more? If you share that attitude, you're missing a valuable, important, and easy avenue to improving employee morale and boosting performance.

Nonmonetary rewards can boost employee performance by motivating workers to repeat the behaviors for which they've been recognized. This can result in workers who feel confident about what they're doing and able to look to the next level of performance or responsibility. An employee who is excited about his job, motivated, and focused on bigger and better things is a satisfied employee, and this translates into employee retention. All those employee traits—satisfied, confident, motivated, and focused on the next level of performance—are good not only for the employee, but the company as well.

Rewarding employees also builds a sense of workplace community by allowing co-workers to see what other employees are doing and achieving.

When to Use Nonmonetary Rewards

When establishing a rewards program, it's important to set some criteria regarding when and why employees will be recognized. Some instances in which you would consider rewarding an employee might include these:

- Somebody comes up with a great idea for saving time or money.

- A customer compliments an employee for providing outstanding service.

- An employee has outstanding attendance and punctuality.

- An employee solves a problem that's been affecting productivity.

- Someone achieves an outstanding achievement, such as the highest sale of the quarter.

- An employee has an outstanding safety record.

- An employee exhibits consistently good performance over time.

When you reward someone, make sure the recipient and other workers know what the reward is for. You also need to establish how often rewards will be given and how an employee will be chosen to receive a reward. Will it be your decision, or can peers nominate one another for recognition?

Making Sure the Reward Makes Sense

Okay, we've established that nonmonetary rewards can be valuable, good for employees and the bottom line. Remember, though, that they've got to be done right in order to be effective. What does that mean, "done right"? It means that nonmonetary rewards must …

- Reflect the goals of the company.
- Be tied to job performance.
- Be fair and consistent.
- Be separate from the employee's pay.

Nonmonetary rewards, ranging from a sincere "thank you," to a half-day off, to a trip to the Bahamas, should be linked to performance and should align with the culture of the company. It doesn't make sense to give somebody a reward, either monetary or nonmonetary, if the intent and purpose of the reward isn't clear.

Let's look at some instances in which it would be appropriate to reward an employee.

Do They Reflect Organizational Goals?

If the goal of your company is to increase sales by 20 percent, it makes sense to reward the employee who closes a major sale with a new client. If your goal is to improve customer service, it makes sense to recognize the employee who makes the extra effort of calling to let a customer know that an order arrived a day early.

If your organizational goal is to reduce its environmental impact by at least 10 percent over three years, by all means reward the team of employees who came up with a plan to arrange for employee carpooling.

When presenting a nonmonetary reward, be sure employees understand exactly what they're being recognized for and how their performance connects to the wider goals of the company. Tell the employee who went out of her way for a customer how those efforts contributed to the goals of the company. Make sure other employees understand as well.

PERFORMANCE GAP

Rewarding someone for something that isn't in step with the goals and direction of the company can be trouble for you, the employee, and the company. If a company goal is to reduce its spending by 15 percent in the next year, for example, an outrageously expensive weekend trip wouldn't be an appropriate reward.

Are They Tied to Job Performance?

You don't want to reward somebody just for showing up or doing what's minimally required. Nonmonetary rewards should be linked directly to job performance, with an obvious tie-in to employee behavior.

Jim was having a difficult time with employees at his service station. They weren't coming in when they were supposed to, they weren't giving customers the kind of service Jim expected them to, they weren't dressing in what Jim considered an appropriate manner—Jim faced all sorts of problems.

Jim's wife, who was probably tired of listening to him complain about the situation, suggested that he initiate a "caught you" program to reward employees who were performing up to or beyond expectations.

Jim warmed up to the idea and spent the next couple days really watching his employees. He made notes about performance gaps he observed, but he also took notice when he saw an employee being extra polite to a customer or picking up litter from the grounds. When he observed an employee going above and beyond the call of duty, he handed that person a little card on which he'd printed "Caught you—thank you!" and a gift card for a local fast-food restaurant. He told employees exactly what he had observed and why he appreciated their actions.

The employees really liked being recognized for providing good service and made a point to do their best. Jim repeats the "caught you" initiate every couple months, giving employees something to look forward to and work toward.

It's important that employees understand both what is expected of them and the parameters for getting a reward. They need to know the criteria on which the rewards will be given.

Are They Fair and Consistent?

While nonmonetary rewards can boost morale and improve employee performance, they can cause problems if they're not given in a fair and consistent manner.

Most employees know what's going on in their workplace. They watch, they talk, and they form opinions. The perception—or even misperception—that a reward has been given unfairly, or wasn't given when it should have been, can cause resentment and hard feelings. That means if Sheila gets a Target gift card as a reward for perfect attendance for the quarter, Nick, who also had perfect attendance, had better get one, too. And they'd better be for the same amount. Fairness and consistency go a long way in all aspects of managing, including when it comes to handing out rewards.

CASE IN POINT

Rasha and Kevin were paired to work together on an important website design project that had to be done on a tight deadline. Rasha jumped in with her usual enthusiasm, staying late to finish and generally doing whatever she could to move the project along. Kevin also acted according to form, refusing to stay past his usual quitting time, texting during work hours, and taking frequent smoke breaks while Rasha worked. The project was completed on time, and in a show of appreciation, Rasha and Kevin got matching gift cards to a popular new restaurant in town. Kevin was pleased with the reward, but Rasha was hurt and furious. She knew she'd contributed far more to completing the project on time than Kevin had. It took months for her to get over the feeling of being treated unfairly.

Are They Separate from Pay?

Nonmonetary rewards have nothing to do with pay. They should never be looked at as a supplement or replacement for pay. For instance, you can't reduce somebody's base pay as part of a cost-saving measure and expect him not to be upset about it because he's in line for free Thanksgiving turkey. Even if the reward would be a week on a tropical island, it wouldn't eliminate the fact that the employee's salary had been reduced.

Also, some employees may feel that nonmonetary rewards are a waste and that the money spent on them would be better spent to increase pay. These employees need to understand that the two have nothing to do with one another and that cutting out nonmonetary gifts would not result in a pay increase.

Using Special Assignments as Rewards

You'll always have employees who want to merely coast along, doing just what's expected of them and nothing more. Those employees will probably view special assignments as impositions, not rewards. But for employees who are motivated and forward looking, special assignments can be powerful and effective rewards. These employees are eager to advance and learn new skills, and special assignments can help them achieve that.

Alicia was assigned a very tedious project of gathering data that her boss needed to prepare a proposal for a client. She spent days making phone calls, looking up statistics and figures, and gathering information. Her boss was thrilled when Alicia presented the information to him on time, in an extremely organized and presentable manner.

Alicia's supervisor was so impressed with her work that, to express his appreciation, he asked her if she wanted to join him when he met with the client. This accomplished several things. The special assignment of visiting a client—something Alicia normally didn't get to do—was a fun and exciting opportunity. It let Alicia see how important her work contribution was to the proposal and how it benefited the company. She was highly motivated by the experience and excited to move on to another project.

Other types of special assignments could include the following:

- A customer visit that involves a trip
- An opportunity to let the employee take your place in a meeting
- Work on a special design project
- Direct contact with customers
- Special training to learn a new task or job
- An opportunity to job-shadow someone in a higher position
- An opportunity to perform a high-profile task or job

Be sure that you consider the likes and dislikes of the employee you're awarding before giving out a special assignment. Offering a customer visit that includes a two-day trip to a single mom or dad with three small children may not be viewed as a reward.

Using Recognition as a Reward

Rewards and recognition go hand in hand. The simple act of recognizing someone for good work can be a powerful reward, and a reward can be a powerful act of recognition.

Many employees feel that their efforts are unrecognized. I hear that over and over when I'm working with them. Some managers, however, don't seem to be able to understand that recognition is necessary. There's nothing weak about thanking someone for a job well done, and it goes a long way toward keeping employees motivated and working at their highest levels.

While a reward is generally something given—a cap, a plaque, or an early quitting time on a Friday, recognition can be as simple as a sincere "thank you." Studies have shown, in fact, that the type of recognition that employees appreciate most is sincere praise that's specific to an act or behavior, and offered in a timely manner. Some companies organize recognition programs that are based on documented achievement and carried out in a specific manner, but there are many informal ways to recognize employees.

> **PERFORMANCE GAP**
>
> If you decide to implement a recognition program, make sure employees fully understand how it will work before you implement it. Most importantly, make sure you carry through with the plan until its scheduled end. Employees will feel abandoned and resentful if a program is abandoned halfway through.

I know an owner of a small company who writes handwritten notes to thank employees who have exceeded expectations. He keeps a box of blank note cards in his desk drawer so he makes the recognition promptly, which is important. It's nothing fancy, but I know for a fact that employees appreciate and keep those cards.

Another way to recognize an employee is to signal him or her out in front of co-workers, letting everyone know what that person has achieved and what it means to the company. You could say, for instance, "I think everyone should know that, because Linda caught that shipping error, we were able to keep the order on track and the customer received it on time. Good job, Linda."

Signaling out Linda in front of her co-workers, as long as she's not very shy and easily embarrassed, is a morale booster for a good employee, and perhaps a motivator for others to perform well. You can recognize employees in lots of ways, many of which don't cost a dime.

What Works for One May Not Work for All

I mentioned earlier that a single parent of small kids might not appreciate a special assignment that requires travel away from home. Employees are motivated by different types of rewards, and you'll need to have a handle on what works for whom in your workplace.

Some employees simply want recognition, while a couple hours off are motivating to someone else. A 50-year-old employee may appreciate a couple tickets to a show or concert more than she would tickets to the hot new club that all the 20-somethings are talking about.

Dan owned a small niche insurance company with about 10 employees. He was a sociable guy, and every couple months he invited his employees to join him for happy hour on a Friday afternoon. Dan intended for the outings to be gestures of appreciation and rewards for good work, but some employees resented what they considered to be extra time spent with their boss and co-workers when they'd rather be home. Although Dan was trying to be a nice guy, he was actually alienating a segment of his employees.

Know Your Employees and Reward Accordingly

Matching appropriate rewards to employees isn't hard if you've taken time to get to know the people who work for you and to consider their likes and dislikes before choosing a reward.

An employee who is working hard to lose weight won't be motivated by or appreciative of coupons for burgers, fries, and soda from the local fast-food place, but another employee who has three kids would probably love them. If you know that Pam and her husband enjoy your city's symphony concerts, by all means recognize her performance with a couple tickets to an upcoming concert.

Let Employees Choose the Rewards

If you're not sure what kinds of nonmonetary rewards will motivate your employees, ask them. Get their input on what works and what doesn't. Better still, give them a budget and let them decide what rewards to offer. Just be sure that they choose a variety of rewards so that something will appeal to everyone. Don't assume that everyone will be thrilled with a company ball cap, since some people don't wear them. Offering a choice between a company ball cap and a company shirt is a better idea.

Alternately, you can come up with a list of rewards on your own and give employees a choice of which they want to receive. Some companies offer a variety of gift cards to national chain stores that employees can choose from. Others allow employees to either start work two hours late or leave two hours early. Allowing your employees to choose the rewards given invests them in the recognition program and generates excitement and workplace loyalty.

Vary Rewards to Avoid the Boredom Factor

Dinner for two, movie tickets, and a special parking place are all fun and appropriate nonmonetary rewards. Employees who receive the same gifts time and time again, however, tend to stop appreciating them so much. When that happens, the rewards no longer motivate your employees to improve their performance.

Some companies offer a different reward every month. One month might be the use of a company car, while the reward the next month is a Home Depot gift card, and a gift certificate to a day spa the month after that. Mixing up employee rewards keeps everyone interested and invested in the program. Employees will talk about what this month's gift is, creating camaraderie and goodwill.

Fifty Innovative and Fun Nonmonetary Rewards

The book *1001 Ways to Reward Employees* (see the Resources appendix) by Bob Nelson has been floating around in the business world for about 10 years and has sold more than 1.4 million copies. Its suggestions for employee rewards range from a bouquet of balloons and pinwheels, to a two-week promotion to the position of special assistant to the company president.

> **CASE IN POINT**
>
> John Sortino is the founder of the Vermont Teddy Bear Company and author of *The Complete Idiot's Guide to Being a Successful Entrepreneur* (Alpha Books, 1999). When the Teddy Bear Company was just starting out and the number of employees was still small, Sortino would reward workers after a particularly busy season, such as Mother's Day, by giving everyone an afternoon off for a picnic and bocce tournament on the company's grounds. Employees loved it, and it required minimal effort and investment on the part of management.

Clearly, there's no shortage of nonmonetary rewards you can use to boost employee performance. Here are 50 inexpensive ideas to get you started. Most of these suggestions are geared toward small businesses. None of them involve a lot of work or are a big deal, just simple ideas to let employees know they're appreciated and valued. You need to decide which ones can work for your business.

1. Create a room where employees recognized for outstanding performance can take a break. Include some snacks, drinks, and a television set.

2. Reward an employee by letting her job-shadow someone in a position of greater authority.

3. Take an employee (or employees) to lunch.

4. Give employees an extra day off before or after a holiday.

5. Throw a latte party, hosted by a local coffee shop.

6. Give away a holiday turkey.

7. Let an employee sit in on a management meeting (when appropriate).

8. Give employees time off for opening day at the beginning of baseball season.

9. Have a frozen treat delivered to the workplace on the first day of spring.

10. Offer use of a company car for a week.

11. Reward viewing privileges for a daytime game if your home baseball team gets to the playoffs or World Series.

12. Provide good-quality company gear for employees to wear.

13. Have a lunchtime pizza party catered by a local pizza shop.

14. Offer an invitation to join you at a Chamber of Commerce mixer or picnic.

15. Offer creative use of the office bulletin board, on which recognized employees get to decide what is posted (assuming it's in good taste, of course).

16. Offer coupons with designated monetary amounts that employees can save up and use to select gifts from catalogues.

17. Institute a "Goal Buster" recognition system with gold stars for employees who exceed performance expectations.

18. Plan a short, informal program in front of peers and management and call out employees who have excelled during the past three months.

19. Give out tickets to a local amusement park.

20. Make a gift to a local charity in the employee's name.

21. Give employees an afternoon off to participate in a community cleanup or painting project.

22. Establish a policy that allows flexible work hours for a week or two for employees who have exceeded goals.

23. Offer the opportunity to share ideas with a team of employees in another area of the company.

24. Give away hard-to-get tickets for a show, concert, or other event.

25. Host a catered breakfast on a Friday morning.

26. Post a note of congratulations or thanks on the employee's office door or cubicle wall.

27. Establish an employee honor roll and post names of those who have exceeded goals.

28. Reward workers who go above and beyond with a pair of tickets to a professional sports event.

29. Hand out trophies or plaques for outstanding service.

30. Provide gift certificates to employees who exceed their goals.

31. Say a sincere "thank you" to an employee who has done something special.

32. Bake or buy cookies and package them in an attractive box to give to employees.

33. Reward team members who have exceeded their goals with a round of golf and an afternoon off to play. Have another activity on tap for nongolfers.

34. Relax the Friday dress code for employees recognized for excellent performance.

35. Reward employees with gift certificates to a local spa.

36. Establish an "employee of the week/month" parking space.

37. Write a note to the employee's spouse or significant other praising his or her performance.

38. Fill a coffee mug bearing the company's logo with hard candy.

39. Hold a monthly celebration to recognize an employee or employees who have exceeded expectations.

40. Establish an "ideas that made a difference" reward that is posted on an office bulletin board or e-mailed to all employees.

41. Allow employees who exceed expectations to accumulate points they can cash in for prizes.

42. Offer hot-air balloon rides to employees who exhibit excellent performance.

43. Reward those who qualify with a laptop bag or briefcase decorated with the company logo.

44. Offer a three- or four-day trip for top achievers.

45. Buy a plant that the employee can keep on his or her desk as a daily reminder of your appreciation.

46. Recognize excellent employees with a 6- or 12-month gym membership.

47. Give a month of free parking to employees who excel.

48. Tie a bunch of brightly colored balloons to the employee's desk or chair.

49. Buy lunch for the employee and three co-workers of his or her choice.

50. Organize a picnic lunch on company grounds.

Remember, it doesn't hurt to give an idea a try. If everyone loves Friday afternoon ice cream parties but there's not an enthusiastic response for amusement park tickets, you'll know what to repeat and what not to.

Is Your Rewards Program Working?

People tend to have short attention spans, and your employees are no exceptions. We get used to something quickly and then start looking for something different. It's important to keep your ear to the ground concerning your rewards and recognition programs.

Programs often start out with great acclaim from employees, only to become ho-hum and taken for granted. I know an employer in a small shop who started handing out candy bars to employees he noticed were working particularly hard or offering to do something that wasn't necessarily expected of them. The candy bars were well received at first. Al would mention to Jack at lunch that he'd had a candy bar that morning. Getting a candy bar was a source of pride. After almost everybody had gotten four or five candy bars, however, the novelty wore off. It wasn't perceived as special anymore, and candy bars started piling up in lockers and on desktops. It was time for a change.

If your employees are excited about a rewards program, you'll hear them talking about it. Look around. Do employees who receive a gift seem excited, or do they take it for granted? If you feel like your rewards program has lost its luster, it's time to ask some questions.

Try to find out whether it's the whole program that isn't working anymore or you just need to switch it up a little bit with different incentives. Remember, there's nothing wrong with putting a rewards and recognition program on hold for a little while, as long as you're up front with employees about what you're doing and why.

If you do that, set a time frame for when the program will be reinstated, and then make sure it is. Let employees know that, although the rewards program has been put on hold, their efforts are still appreciated. You can do that simply by sincerely thanking employees for jobs well done.

The Least You Need to Know

- Nonmonetary rewards motivate and recognize employees.
- You have access to a wide range of nonmonetary rewards, but all should go above and beyond a paycheck.
- Tailor rewards to each employee.
- Reward programs sometimes outlive their usefulness and should be reevaluated from time to time.

Why Delegate?

In This Chapter

- You can't grow your business all by yourself
- How delegating boosts your bottom line
- Using delegation to boost performance
- Knowing when and what to delegate
- Making delegation work for you and your team

Many managers want to do it all—especially if the business they manage is their own. If you're running your own business, it's easy to adopt an attitude of, "It's my business, and I'll run it the way I want to run it."

Sometimes that approach is okay, especially if you have extensive business experience, but in most cases, it won't get you very far. Running a business is a communal activity. Almost all businesses require the efforts of more than one person. A business has employees, customers, suppliers, and salespeople—and all those people are necessary in keeping the operation running smoothly.

As difficult as it is for some managers to understand, others often bring different perspectives to the business, along with some great ideas. That's why smart managers and business owners understand that running a business isn't a one-person job, and they learn to share and delegate authority and responsibility.

In this chapter, you'll learn why it's important to delegate and how to do it so that you, your employees, and your business will benefit.

Why You Need to Be Able to Delegate

The simple fact is that one person can't do it all, and if you try to, you and your business will suffer. Some managers don't delegate, because they honestly believe no one else can do the job as well as they can. That may or may not be the case, but refusing to delegate work to employees doesn't say much for your confidence in their abilities—or the role you've played in developing those abilities.

If you've followed the steps of the performance management cycle by establishing job performance standards and expectations, providing effective training and coaching, and reviewing performance, your employees should be perfectly capable of achieving the tasks you delegate.

Other managers are afraid it will appear that they're slacking off or can't handle their work if they delegate. The truth is, however, if the workload is more than you're able to effectively handle, the quality of the work will suffer and negatively affect the organization. Being willing and able to delegate work indicates your understanding of the needs of the company and how those needs are best accomplished.

PERFORMANCE BOOST

The work you delegate doesn't always have to be your own. If you notice an employee who's struggling with too much work, delegate some of it to another team member who might be looking for something to do.

A key advantage of delegating work is that it keeps the workload of your department or organization evenly distributed and avoids the possibility that some workers will be sitting around while others carry the load. When you delegate work, be sure to include everyone and spread the work among all employees.

You'll always have some employees who are willing to take on more than others. They may be more confident in their abilities, be actively working toward advancement in the company, or simply possess higher energy levels than others. Resist the temptation to hand off unrealistic amounts of work to those employees, who eventually will become frustrated and burned out if you do.

I've worked with a lot of managers on the issue of delegating work and have noticed some common excuses for not doing it. Let's take a minute to think about each of these excuses and figure out why they don't hold up.

It's Easier to Do It Myself

Although it might take longer for you to explain a task and show someone how to perform it than it would for you to do it yourself, you'll soon have the employee trained and yourself freed up for other jobs. Investing a little time in establishing performance expectations and training for a particular job is well worth the time and effort it will save you in the future.

Consider an example. I worked with Jim, who complained repeatedly about having to put together a daily report for a supervisor. It took him only about a half hour a day, but he had to do it every day. He said he'd love to delegate the task, but it would take too long to train somebody and was easier just to do himself. I asked Jim how long he thought he'd have to work with an employee before he could turn over the job completely, and he said he thought it would take about four hours of training. I pointed out that he spent two and a half hours a week on these reports, and, if he started training now, in just four hours he'd no longer have to worry about them. At 10 hours of work per month, Jim would save 116 hours in the first year alone by investing 4 hours in preparing someone to take over the job.

Reluctance to Overload Employees

Employees do have their own work, that's true. When asked to take on additional responsibilities, however, most employees will be flattered and motivated. When you delegate work, you also delegate responsibility—and your confidence that employees are capable of rising to the occasion and doing what needs to be done.

Entrepreneurs who start their own businesses sometimes have the most trouble delegating work to employees. That attitude is understandable because of their sense of ownership and responsibility, but it can be counterproductive. Taking on the roles of manager, laborer, business manger, marketing person, and custodian might work for a short time, but it isn't a sustainable way of running a business. There's a reason you have employees, even if it's just one or two, so resist the temptation to do it all by yourself.

Fear of Employee Failure

Employees will make mistakes, but you will, too. There's no guarantee that a job will get completed without any problems, regardless of who is performing it. If a problem does occur with work you've delegated, chances are, your superior will welcome the news that you're creating an even work distribution in your department, not chastise you.

Loss of Control

The fear of losing control by delegating work is widespread but largely ungrounded. You're the manager. When you delegate jobs, you don't do so without follow-through. You don't hand off work to someone and then forget about it. By checking in with employees and providing feedback, you stay right on top of how work is progressing and minimize the potential for any problems that might occur. Your time and energy is better spent distributing the workload and making sure everyone has something to do than trying to do it all yourself.

If you're not comfortable with delegating work, you need to consider all of the advantages of doing so and come up with a plan for how you'll begin.

Delegating work that someone else can do gives you more time to deal with bigger issues within your department or company, and to focus on the organization's goals and mission.

Delegate to Boost the Bottom Line

Delegating work increases productivity, which boosts the company's bottom line. Motivated, productive workers accomplish more than those who are not, and that's good for you, for them, and for the company.

Delegating work also frees up some of your time to take on important tasks such as working to increase sales, boosting your marketing efforts, calling on potential customers, or following up with current customers.

Consider the return on investment you get by performing certain jobs or tasks. It might take you an hour to organize product for shipping. If an employee can assume that task successfully, you have an extra hour to spend on a task with a greater return on investment potential, such as calling the prospective customer you met last week and setting up an appointment.

CASE IN POINT

Julia is a human resources manager in a busy health care setting. After her department experienced layoffs, everyone worked harder to handle the extra work. Knowing that her employees were already assuming more responsibility, Julia was reluctant to delegate any work. The problem was that Julia's supervisor wasn't reluctant to delegate a lot of his increasing workload to her. Julia became overwhelmed and considered looking for another job when her supervisor became aware of the situation. They were able to work out a plan for Julia to delegate some of her nonessential work to members of her department. Most of her employees understood the situation and were willing to help out, and Julia was able to more effectively handle her responsibilities without feeling overwhelmed.

When you delegate some of your own work to qualified employees, you create more time for yourself without overburdening your team. Your employees get the opportunity to increase skills and knowledge, which improves their chances for career advancement. Performance also increases due to motivated workers and high productivity.

How Delegating Work Boosts Performance

It's not hard to recognize employees who are engaged in and excited about their jobs. They like to try new methods of performing tasks, they ask questions, and they express ideas. Experienced managers recognize that these employees are valuable assets to the department.

Delegating work and responsibilities to these employees tends to feed into their enthusiasm and result in further engagement and ownership. They are challenged to handle the additional responsibility successfully, and their performance levels increase.

However, the benefits of delegating work and responsibility are not always limited to your high-performance employees. Workers who are content to do only what they need to, coasting along without expressing much interest or enthusiasm about their work, often benefit from delegation as much as their more motivated counterparts.

Some employees who are initially reluctant to take on extra work surprise themselves by performing better than they thought they could. When that occurs, confidence levels increase and employees may look for other opportunities to advance their skills and knowledge. Some employees discover new areas of interest, which is exciting and increases productivity. In time, these employees may join their motivated peers in coming up with ideas of their own and may welcome their increased responsibilities. You might be very surprised to learn that some employees are capable of handling certain tasks even better than you!

Encourages Responsibility and Ownership

Most employees enjoy some level of responsibility within their jobs and want to feel proud about what they do. They want to own their jobs by being given the opportunity to offer input and come up with ways to improve the job. Delegating work to these employees increases their responsibility level, along with their motivation and performance levels.

Allows Employees to Learn New Skills and Gain Experience

Many workplaces in the current economic environment are finding it necessary to ask employees to assume more work, meaning it's necessary for them to learn new skills. While some employees might resent this, others will find it to be exciting and challenging.

Employees who learn new skills make themselves more valuable to the workplace, meaning they're more likely to retain their jobs and advance in them. Delegating work that gives employees these opportunities is advantageous to both you and them. Be sure to explain the advantages of employee enrichment when delegating to less-than-enthusiastic employees.

Provides Recognition

Everyone likes to be recognized for their work. When you delegate work to an employee, be sure others know that job assignments have changed and which employee will be taking on additional responsibilities. This gives recognition to the person to whom you're delegating work, while at the same time providing incentive for others to look for additional responsibility. In time, you can create an atmosphere in which employees who don't get extra work feel left out and actually seek more responsibility in order to be recognized.

What to Delegate and What Not to Delegate

While it makes sense to delegate many tasks and jobs, in some instances, delegation isn't a good idea. Let's take a look at the types of work to delegate and the types of jobs that should remain with you.

Consider delegating these kinds of jobs:

- **Tasks that don't require your level of skill.** There's no point in you sorting papers or answering the phone when someone else can perform those tasks without any problem. Handing off these jobs frees you up for jobs that require higher levels of expertise and are more valuable to the organization.

- **Jobs that require skills you don't possess.** Unless you're trained and qualified to prepare business tax returns, delegate that job to someone with the appropriate set of skills, such as a business accountant.

- **Low-priority tasks.** If a job is near the bottom of your to-do list, chances are, it's a low-priority task that can be delegated to someone else. Just be sure it isn't so low priority that it's actually unnecessary.

- **Jobs that others have been trained to do.** If you enjoy handling customer concerns but you have customer service representatives who are trained for that job, it's probably best to leave that work to them and identify a job for which you are uniquely qualified.

Examples of the types of jobs you shouldn't delegate include these:

- **Jobs on which the future of the company depends.** That might be overly dramatic, but if it's a really, really important task, it's probably best to do it yourself. That not only increases the probability that the job will be done properly, but it also eliminates the burden to an employee of having to handle such an important task.

- **Jobs that involve sensitive or confidential information.** These jobs could include writing proposals or processing information concerning salary, employment matters, or customers. Don't delegate any job that entails something of a sensitive nature.

- **Tasks assigned specifically to you.** If your supervisor asked you to speak about your job to her son's eighth-grade class on career day, that's not a job you want to delegate to somebody else. You should handle a job that was assigned to you for a particular reason.

- **High-priority tasks.** Just as low-priority jobs are at the bottom of your to-do list for a reason, high-priority tasks are at the top because they need to be done now and done right. Handle these jobs yourself.

- **Jobs involving a difficult customer.** If you know that a customer is extremely hard to please or there's been a problem in the past, it's probably best for you to handle the task. Chances are, you'd be forced to get involved anyway if the customer was dissatisfied again.

In most cases, deciding whether to delegate a job is a judgment call that you'll need to make. You'll get a better sense of what your employees are willing and able to do once you begin the process of delegating.

How to Delegate

When you've made the decision to delegate work in order to relieve some of your burden and provide employees with opportunities for increased skills and possible advancement, you have to decide how you'll go about the actual task of dividing up and assigning the work.

Delegating work isn't something you should do without consideration or planning, because if you don't get it right the first time, employees likely won't think it's a good idea the next time around.

PERFORMANCE BOOST

If you're delegating well, you will be satisfied with the way employees perform their jobs, and employees will feel committed and involved. Morale within the workplace will be high. If you're not delegating properly, you'll find that you have way too much to do and you're spending too much time on details. This could cause problems for you when it's time for your performance evaluation because you're not able to perform your job as effectively as you should. With improper delegation, employees will feel discontented because they won't feel challenged or fulfilled, and you may face a turnover problem.

Basically, you should follow these steps when delegating work:

1. Decide which jobs you'll delegate. Use the information from the previous section to determine which jobs you'll hand off and which you'll keep for yourself.

2. Identify employees for different jobs. Consider demonstrated skill, employee motivation, workload, and desire to grow within the organization, among other qualities.

3. Establish performance standards and expectations for the job to be delegated. Review Chapter 2—your employees need to know what to do, how to do it, and why they're doing it. Be as specific as you can and provide adequate information regarding the job.

4. Identify resources and authority. Will this job require resources, such as additional personnel or money, that the employee may not have? Will the employee be given the authority necessary to complete the task, such as to request funds or ask for additional help?

5. Identify possible complications. If you know of any particular challenges associated with the job you're delegating, be sure to let your employees know. If an employee will need to be dealing with someone who's difficult to work with, for instance, it's best to share that ahead of time.

6. Establish how job performance will be evaluated. Will you check in with the employee every day? Weekly? Do you expect written progress reports?

7. Make sure you and your employee share the same expectations regarding the work to be delegated. Spend some time discussing your understanding and expectations, and ask your employee to express expectations and concerns as well.

Delegation Planning Worksheet

Use the following planning worksheet to help ensure that your efforts to delegate work are successful.

1. Briefly describe the job you want to delegate.

_____

_____

_____

2. Name the person to whom you will delegate the work.

_____

3. Describe any special preparation the person is likely to need (for example, classroom or one-on-one training or coaching).

_____

_____

_____

4. Briefly list the essential information you need to convey to the person who will do the job.

_____

_____

_____

Overview of what the job involves:

_____

_____

_____

Reasons the job is important:

_____

_____

_____

Results you expect:

_____

_____

_____

Deadlines and scope of authority:

_____

_____

_____

Decide together on check-in times to ensure that the job stays on track:

_____

_____

_____

Don't Set Someone Up to Fail

When delegating work, it's extremely important to be sure that the employee's skills are up to the task. Handing over a job to someone who's not qualified to handle it isn't fair or productive, and will only make the employee feel frustrated and inadequate.

Also be sure that the employee has the time necessary to take on additional work. If possible, try to match work with employee interests. If you need someone to proofread proposals, for instance, and you know that Donna enjoys proofreading and is good at it, it wouldn't make sense to pass that task on to Dan, who dislikes anything that involves reading.

PERFORMANCE GAP

While assigning someone a job that's beyond their abilities will result in frustration, delegating work that's way below someone's abilities can cause boredom and resentment. Setting up someone to fail can be an unintended result of expecting either too much or too little of an employee.

If you're considering delegating a particular job and you're not sure whether the employee you have in mind is capable of it, ask what he or she thinks. If the employee is the likely candidate for the job and isn't confident about handling it, make sure he or she gets some training to increase confidence and ensure success. When the employee begins the job, keep a close eye on him or her until you're satisfied that it's progressing smoothly.

The Least You Need to Know

- Delegating work is a skill that benefits both you and your employees.
- Delegation boosts performance, morale, and productivity.
- Certain types of tasks are more appropriate for delegation than others.
- Delegating work requires thought and preparation.

Leadership Challenges

The best managers possess the qualities of flexibility, the ability to think on their feet, and a good sense of humor. The business world is full of challenges, and leaders must be ready to rise to meet them, while at the same time keeping their employees on track. Part 5 provides an overview of leadership styles to help you figure out how you lead and then provides direction for leading employees of all ages during hard times and good times.

Leadership Style

In This Chapter

- Defining leadership style
- The four basic styles of leadership
- Knowing which leadership style to use
- Employee problem—or leadership problem?
- Trusting your instincts when choosing a style
- Leadership techniques to strive for

You hear a lot about leadership style, but often in the context of determining your natural leadership style or figuring out what kind of leader you are. Truth be told, your natural leadership style isn't all that important. Although that's the style you'll use in some cases, and perhaps the style you'll fall into when you have to react quickly to a situation, you really need to cultivate other styles as well and learn when it's appropriate to use each of them.

In this chapter, you'll learn about four basic leadership styles: directing, coaching, participating, and delegating. You'll also learn the circumstances in which each of those styles works and should be employed.

What Is Leadership Style?

Your leadership style is simply the manner in which you work with people. It's how you approach your leadership role and how you interact with your employees. It's closely linked to motivating employees and boosting performance, and it's certainly worth your consideration.

CASE IN POINT

We've known about leadership style for a long time. It was first studied in the late 1930s when a psychologist named Kurt Lewin led a study on leadership that identified three different, general styles and the responses they drew. Interestingly, the three styles identified—authoritarian, democratic, and *laissez-faire*—were tested on groups of children, whom leaders led in an arts and crafts project. Three leaders, each employing one of those leadership styles, led groups of children while researchers watched their responses. Additional leadership styles have been identified since then, but Lewin's study remains an important part of management history.

Your primary leadership style, or the one to which you'll gravitate when you don't have time to figure out which style might work best, results from a variety of influences.

It's thought that influences early in your life affect your leadership style. That's because we tend to base our preferences on childhood experiences. If you had a parent who was very nurturing, for instance, you might tend toward a coaching style of leadership. If your parent was authoritative and your household was run in a strict manner, you might lean toward a directing style.

The styles of supervisors you experienced in early jobs also may have had an effect on your leadership tendencies, as will the culture of the company you work for presently. Your style also depends on your employees and the work they're expected to perform.

When you read over the descriptions of the four basic leadership styles in the next section—others have added still more—you can determine which comes most naturally to you. It probably won't be difficult for you to do, because you probably already have an idea of how you lead, even if you never put a name to it.

Over the years, I've identified five fundamental principles of leadership that I believe are essentially important for managers. In no particular order, they are:

- Transfer ownership.
- Create an environment for ownership where each person wants to be responsible.
- Coach the development of personal capabilities.
- Learn faster and encourage others to do the same.
- Focus on great performance for your customers.

Basic Leadership Styles and When to Use Them

It's important to understand that one leadership style is not better or worse than another, although one will work better or worse than another in a particular situation and with a particular worker or group. The critical issue is to be familiar enough with all four styles so you can switch from one to another when necessary.

Let's look at each style so you can hear what it sounds like, when it's generally effective to use, and when it's the wrong way to go.

Directing

The directing style of leadership does just what the name implies: it provides direction. It sounds like, "This is how it needs to be done," and it's a very effective style in some cases.

The directing style works with new or inexperienced employees who require supervision and need to be told what to do. It's valuable when new procedures are being established or when an employee needs specific direction and follow-up attention.

It's also good in an emergency, when it's necessary for someone to take charge and provide direction for others. Directing is often the best response if you're challenged by an employee, and it's often used as a transitional style for employees who have been poorly managed and are not meeting performance expectations.

This style doesn't work well, however, with employees who are highly motivated and already meeting or exceeding expectations, or those who know their jobs well and don't require a lot of supervision or direction. In those cases, this leadership style is usually perceived as the behavior of a bossy manager who likes to throw his weight around.

Coaching

Like directing, the coaching leadership style is hands-on. It sounds like, "Next time, be sure that you check the sales sheet before sending out the orders."

The coaching style works with employees who know their jobs but require some adjustments and improvements in the way they perform them. This style is effective when some corrective action is needed or when an employee is struggling with a particular task and needs some extra help. It also reinforces good performance, which is motivating to employees.

As with the directing style, the coaching style isn't effective with accomplished workers who are self-motivated and want to perform their jobs in the manner that works best for them. In those cases, it comes off as being heavy-handed and intrusive rather than helpful.

PERFORMANCE GAP

Some leadership styles require more time and patience than others. Taking time out to solicit employees' ideas and input is useful and can be a real performance booster, but if you're up against a huge deadline and every second counts, it's not appropriate for the situation. You have to match your leadership style not only to your employees, but to your job circumstances as well. If you don't, you could end up frustrating both yourself and your employees.

Participating

The participating leadership style uses "we" instead of "I" or "you," and is team oriented. It involves asking employees for their input and sounds something like, "How do you think we could do this better?"

The participating leadership style is effective with experienced employees who possess good knowledge of the job and employees who are eager to share their ideas. If there's a complex decision to be made and you're confident that input from employees is valuable or necessary, this is the leadership style to go with.

The participating leadership style isn't effective when there are tight time constraints or if employees aren't interested in getting involved. Because this method of leadership can be time consuming, it doesn't make sense to employ it for every small decision or action.

Delegating

As you read in Chapter 19, delegating is a strong management technique that can contribute to boosting employee performance. It's also a great leadership style in certain instances. The delegating style of management sounds like, "Could you please handle this project?" and it carries a number of advantages.

Experienced employees who have a real grasp on the job and are motivated by "ownership" respond well to this leadership style. These employees are typically your top performers, those you know you can count on. In addition to motivating them even further, this style can free you up for other tasks, or for working with employees who require extra attention.

Clearly, this leadership style is not beneficial with employees you can't depend on or those without adequate skills or knowledge to get the job done correctly.

You can find online tests and quizzes to help you determine your leadership style, but after reading these descriptions, you probably have a pretty good idea of what comes most naturally to you. Take the quizzes if you want (the Small Business Administration provides one at www.sba. gov/smallbusinessplanner/manage/lead/SERV_MGMTSTYLE.html), but remember that you need to cultivate all leadership styles to meet the needs and fit the personalities of all your employees.

Is It an Employee Problem or a Leadership Problem?

Have you ever had one (or more) of those employees who just don't seem to get it? You tell someone over and over again what you want him to do, and he stands there scratching his head? Well, he just may not be that great of an employee. Or maybe he's just not responding to your leadership style.

I've seen this again and again with managers who don't understand that a leadership style that works well with some employees doesn't work well with others. Managers who don't know how to match their leadership style to the needs of their employees—or simply aren't interested in doing so—will not get the best from their workers.

CASE IN POINT

Brianna worked in the produce department at a store that's part of a regional grocery chain. Her job was to restock and arrange the produce, handle returns of unsellable goods, and work with customers who had questions or needed help. The produce manager told her repeatedly what to do, but Brianna never quite got it right. The manager was frustrated, and Brianna was constantly stressed out, waiting for the next reprimand. Finally, after some training on leadership style, the manager realized that Brianna wasn't responding to being told what to do. Once he adopted a coaching style and took the time to provide some hands-on help, she responded well and her job performance improved tremendously.

If you have an employee, or more than one, who is not performing up to expectations, try adjusting your leadership style and see what happens. Evaluate the employee so you can effectively use one of the leadership styles described earlier. If you've been using a coaching style and it isn't working, your employee might be feeling stifled or might think that you're being condescending. Try a participating style. You might be pleasantly surprised with the results.

If you're stuck on which leadership style to use with a particular employee, try asking what he or she prefers. You wouldn't, of course, ask whether the employee prefers that you use a participating style of leadership over a directing style. But you ask whether he or she prefers to see more of you during the day or less of you. Does the employee like the thought of taking a job and running with it? Does the employee appreciate it when you work with him and/or demonstrate how something needs to be done?

Being willing to work with employees to determine the leadership style they respond to best will pay off handsomely as their performances improve and your workplace runs smoothly.

Go with Your Gut

There's no surefire way to know which leadership style will be most effective with every employee, especially those you haven't gotten a chance to know very well. Sometimes you have to test the waters, trying out a style and then flexing it if it doesn't seem to be effective. And sometimes you have to switch styles in the middle of the stream. Managing employees has a lot in common with raising kids. To get much accomplished, you have to be flexible and willing to work with them.

PERFORMANCE BOOST

Be proactive about switching your leadership style. If you sense that a style isn't working, don't wait until both you and your employee are frustrated and irritated before you try a different one.

If a teenager is rushing to get through chores before she leaves for a shopping excursion with friends, she might respond well to a directing style of parenting. Just tell her what to do so she can finish up and leave. On a day when she's feeling relaxed and has some time on her hands, she might be receptive to a little coaching. And on a day when she's a little moody because she thinks you're always criticizing her and nobody appreciates her, she just might require a participating style.

The same goes with employees. If Brad is having a bad day and you approach him with a delegating style of leadership, he might feel put upon and overburdened, whereas on another day, he'd welcome being asked to take over a job.

These are the times, just as with parenting, that you need to trust your gut and approach the employee in a manner that you feel is appropriate for the particular circumstances. If you find that you're wrong, switch your style. The trick is to get familiar enough with each of the four styles so that you can move in and out of them without having to think much about it.

Tough Love

When all else fails, tough love is a leadership technique to consider. Tough love becomes necessary when, for whatever reasons, an employee with valuable skills has not been performing well for a period of time. You've exhausted all other options, from coaching to written warnings, with no success. You'd like to see this employee turn things around because, frankly, he's experienced and his skills are needed. You're reluctant to fire him because he'd be hard to replace, but his poor performance is impacting others and the business. Give the employee a retreat day—one day off with pay—to consider whether he wants to remain an employee and, if so, to come up with a 30-day plan for how he's going to improve. You and he review the plan and agree to it, and then you see whether he carries it through. If not, you need to say goodbye to that employee. Tough love is just that, tough, but it sometimes is the only tool you've got left in your box. If that's the case, use it.

Leadership Techniques to Strive For

Regardless of what you perceive to be your natural leadership style, you need to be adaptable and willing to change the style you use to meet the needs of employees.

Managers who want to get the most from their employees, and are willing to work with them to ensure that it happens, are open to practicing different leadership styles and being flexible in which ones they use.

Effective managers also practice other leadership techniques that result in healthy morale and boost employee performance. Check out the following questions, and be honest with yourself about your answers. Just answer "yes" or "no" to each question. This isn't a test on your leadership abilities; it's merely an exercise to get you thinking about your leadership style and the level to which you're involved with your team.

- Do you set clear and specific goals for your employees?
- Do you find ways to empower your employees?
- Do you solicit ideas from your employees?
- Do you delegate tasks that will develop your employees?
- Do you take time to coach employees?
- Do you give timely and accurate feedback to your employees?
- Do you solicit feedback from your employees about your leadership performance?
- Do you recognize and reward good performance?
- Do you address performance gaps in a timely manner?
- Do you adjust your leadership style based on the needs of the individual and the group?
- Do you communicate effectively in both verbal and written communications?

- Do you actively listen to and show genuine interest in your employees?

- Do you involve employees in decision making that affects them?

- Do you maintain a calm, steady demeanor, even in stressful situations?

- Do you continually seek ways to improve as a leader?

Of all these questions, the last one well may be the most important. There are no perfect leaders, just as there are no perfect employees. It makes no sense, however, to expect your employees to be willing to work to improve their performance if you're not doing the same.

PERFORMANCE BOOST

Smart managers know that it's okay—and healthy—to focus on the human side of their employees. To do this, keep these tips in mind:

- Make your people feel important.
- Show that you care.
- Understand the person behind the employee.
- Reward your employee's efforts.
- Encourage two-way conversation.

Effective leadership is a process, and it takes work to achieve and maintain it. You can always learn more and get better at managing employees. All it takes is a willingness to do so. So think about the questions to which you answered "no," and then think about what work you need to do to improve in those areas.

The Least You Need to Know

- Leadership styles are developed over time and influenced by different sources.

- Determine which style comes most naturally to you, but be willing to practice all four styles.

- Sometimes an employee problem turns out to be a leadership problem.

- Striving for continual improvement might be the most important quality of good management.

Get the Best from Employees

In This Chapter

- One size does not fit all
- Understanding traits and characteristics of four generations
- What employees want and expect
- Forgetting about the golden rule

When you really think about it, it's a wonder that our workplaces are as successful and productive as many are. In addition to unprecedented competition from all over the world, a global recession that has resulted in downsizing and cuts of every kind imaginable, threats of terrorism and other causes for constant stress, and immigration issues affecting workers, for the first time in America, four generations of employees are working together.

Maybe I should say that four generations are at least *trying* to work together. Relationships between generations can be difficult, and they may become more so as the rules are changing rapidly. These intergenerational relationships and the challenges that come with them aren't limited to employment situations. They also occur among parents and children, older and younger politicians—nearly any arena in which people of generations interact. In this chapter, we examine the four generations that are competing for and sharing jobs in U.S. workplaces, and we look at how smart managers are learning to accommodate all of them to keep their businesses running smoothly and keep their employees motivated.

How to Manage Employees of Every Age

If you're 44 and a manager, you could have team members who are the ages of both your parents and your kids. If you're a whiz kid manager at age 23, you could be in charge of employees who are the ages of your parents and grandparents. If you're a manager at 65, you could be managing peers of your kids and grandkids.

If you think that a one-size-fits-all management style will work in any of those circumstances, think again. To successfully manage the workers of four different generations currently in the workplace, you have to take into consideration how members of each generation communicate, the way they get work done, their attitudes regarding work, their values, the way they use technology, their ideas about how things should go, and many other attributes.

PERFORMANCE BOOST

It helps to remember that every generation caused a stir as it entered the working world. It's human nature to think that your way is the best way and that everyone else should follow along, but older workers need to learn to accommodate younger ones, and vice versa.

If you're the 44-year-old manager, you surely understand that there's no way a worker who is your parent's age has the same values, attitudes, and ideas regarding work and how it should get done as an employee who is the approximate age of your son or daughter. And that's not even mentioning the differences in attitudes and aptitudes regarding technology and electronics.

Managing employees has always been tricky business for the very reason that you're dealing with people. These days more than ever, however, you need to consider the needs and wants of your team members of all ages if you expect them to be motivated and productive workers.

Let's take a look at the four generations currently in our workplaces and examine some of the personal and work-related characteristics of each.

The Generations

Five different sources may provide five different age ranges and names for the four generations we're dealing with. All of those sources would agree that certain characteristics correspond to each one. So while you might not agree on the starting and stopping dates for the generations we'll be discussing, you still can get a big-picture overview of the characteristics that apply to people born within, or close to within, those dates.

In a nutshell, you'll be reading about the following generations:

- **Veterans.** This is the generation born between 1922 and 1945. In normal times there wouldn't be too many of these warriors left in the workplace, but their presence has increased due to a considerable number of people who are delaying retirement or re-entering the work force because of tough economic times. Under any circumstances, their influence is still widely felt. Also known as the Matures or the Greatest Generation, they are defined as disciplined and respectful of authority. Honor is extremely important to them. For many in this generation, education was a commodity to be pursued, a dream.

   Many of the Greatest Generation were children of the Great Depression, and teens or young adults during World War II and the Korean War. They grew up in traditional families. Technology can be problematic for members of this generation, and their attitude toward money tends to lean toward saving what you can and paying cash for what you buy.

- **Baby Boomers.** Born between 1946 and 1964, Baby Boomers are still going strong in the workplace. Despite the fact that they're nearing, or have reached, traditional retirement age, many have no intention of leaving, due to ailing retirement funds caused by stock market woes or inadequate savings. This can cause hard feelings among younger workers, who feel that the Boomers are holding them back.

Boomers, many of whom considered education to be a right instead of a privilege, tend to be optimistic and involved in their communities. The first generation to regularly and comfortably use credit cards for purchase, they have a "buy now and pay later" attitude. Many have embraced technology, although some still are wary. Events and experiences that have shaped this generation include the Cold War, early space travel, the sexual revolution, assassinations, and the Civil Rights movement. Members of this generation have witnessed the onset of technology in the form of computers and other electronics, having grown up without computers or the Internet.

- **Generation X.** Born between 1965 and 1980, Gen Xers have fewer members than the preceding two generations and the one that follows. Their early years occurred during a relatively peaceful time, but they were influenced by events such as Watergate, women's liberation, the energy crisis, and Desert Storm, and were affected by high divorce rates among their parents.

  Members of Generation X tend to be skeptical and wary, but they love to have fun. They are informal in their dealings, cautious and conservative with money, and used to being on their own as latch-key kids. They view education as a means to an end and are comfortable with technology.

- **Generation Y.** Also known as the Millennials, this generation was born between 1980 and 1990. Technology has been a major factor in their lives, and many have grown up with overprotective parents, determined to protect and enhance their children's self-esteem and provide for not only all of their needs, but all of their wants as well. They've also been influenced by events such as school shootings, commonplace political scandals, and corruption in other areas.

  They trend toward being realistic and confident, along with extremely social and fun seeking. They've grown up in merged families and are influenced by, among other things, 9/11, social networking, and technology. Their opinion on education is that, although it's necessary, it's an incredible burden because of the expense, and they tend to earn money in order to spend money.

While these are very general characteristics, they give you an idea of how different members of these generations can be.

Now let's look at the attitudes and values that affect each of these generations at work. As you know, not every member of these different generations possesses all the characteristics mentioned. However, the results of many studies support these general patterns that apply to generations.

People born in the first or last years of a particular generation may possess some of the traits that define their own generation, along with those of the generation before or after their own.

Veterans

Veterans tend to be good workers, in that they work hard, are willing to make sacrifices for their jobs, follow rules, respect authority, and put duty before fun. They consider work to be an obligation, and they keep it separate from their family and personal lives.

All of those traits, while admirable, can be annoying to younger employees, who may view their older counterparts as being overly serious and lacking in imagination and spontaneity. On the flip side, Veterans, or members of the Greatest Generation, sometimes consider younger workers to be too glib about work, poor communicators, and unable to focus. Members of this generation who are managers tend to be very directive and use a command-and-control style.

Baby Boomers

Baby Boomers are accustomed to working until a job is finished, sometimes at the expense of their personal or family lives. They look at work as an adventure, not an obligation, and they are characterized as being efficient workers who seek personal fulfillment from what they do. They value quality work and aren't afraid to question authority or champion for causes they consider to be important.

Baby Boomers like meetings, and they tend to be team players, which can alienate them from younger workers who prefer e-mail or voice mail to gatherings. As mentioned earlier, Boomers have become an annoyance to some members of generations X and Y, who are impatiently waiting to move up the ladder and fill the jobs they feel should be theirs instead of occupied by aging Baby Boomers who are unable, or unwilling, to retire.

PERFORMANCE BOOST

Even before serious economic troubles became apparent near the end of 2007, attitudes toward retirement were changing. The average retirement age in the early 1960s was 66, but it kept dropping over the years to a point that it reached 62 years. However, many people who retired at age 62 found themselves feeling alienated and depressed. They returned to work, either full-time or part-time, and enjoyed both the additional income and the feeling of connection and worth.

Generation X

Members of Generation X value structure at work and seek direction, but they tend to be self-reliant and skeptical, which sometimes leads to conflict. An older manager could provide direction regarding a project at the request of a Gen X employee, only to have the employee reply with something like, "Well, I could do that, but I'm not sure how well it would work."

Gen Xers view work as a difficult challenge and something that they've contracted to do. They prefer to interact in an entrepreneurial style, by consulting and planning with others in an informal manner, and they seek a work/life balance. Managers of this generation tend to treat everyone in the same manner, challenge their employees, and question what they do and why.

Generation Y

Members of this generation grew up listening to music as they worked on laptops, texted friends, and sent e-mails, so they're used to multitasking. They tend to be goal oriented and tenacious about reaching those goals, while at the same time looking to the next task. Members of Generation Y are citizens of the world and tend to be tolerant of others. They view work as both fulfilling and a means to an end.

Older co-workers sometimes view members of this generation as being unfocused and spoiled, and in need of constant attention. They can be challenging to managers because they can't be bothered by meetings or mundane tasks, even when those tasks are necessary. However, they are loyal and curious, and they share many of the same traits of the Veteran generation.

What Workers of Different Ages Expect from You

More than anything, workers of different ages expect you to treat them in an age-appropriate manner. They do not, and will not, appreciate a one-size management style. An older employee, for instance, may not appreciate a young manager calling him by his first name or giving him a nickname.

It also means that you might need to hover a little bit over your youngest workers and give them a good deal of feedback. Members of Generation Y, if you'll recall, grew up with constant positive reinforcement and some of them feel lost without it.

Generally, you should keep these considerations in mind when managing workers of varying ages:

- The method in which they prefer to communicate and interact with co-workers and managers
- The type of feedback that motivates them
- The type of rewards they value
- The messages that will motivate them
- Their views on work/family/personal life balance

Let's look at each of those topics and consider the expectations of each generation.

Communication and Personal Interaction

The Greatest Generation wants a memo or formal announcement of a communication, while Baby Boomers prefer to be consulted in person. Members of Generation X expect communication to be immediate—they need to know now. They also do not appreciate receiving second-hand information and prefer to be informed directly.

Those in Generation Y don't want to be interrupted or bothered by communication; they'd rather deal with it by e-mail, voice mail, or text message.

Regarding personal interaction, Veterans prefer a one-on-one approach, while Baby Boomers like a team approach and value meetings.

Throwing around ideas and brainstorming with others appeals to members of Generation X, but they prefer to do so in a more casual manner than in meetings, perhaps over lunch or during an informal sit-down in someone's office.

Members of Generation Y prefer participatory interaction, and they want their opinions and thoughts to be acknowledged and taken seriously.

CASE IN POINT

Terry was a stuck-in-the-middle manager of a small manufacturing operation. At age 44, he managed employees who were both significantly older and significantly younger than he. When Terry stated expectations for a job, his older employees generally nodded, maybe took some notes, and got to work. The younger employees, however, often questioned why they were expected to perform a particular task or why they should do the job in the manner Terry had specified. This was frustrating at first to Terry and annoying to the older employees, who considered the behavior disrespectful. Some HR training taught Terry that the younger workers had been taught to question and that doing so was practically their obligation. Terry communicated this to the older workers and encouraged them to also voice questions or concerns.

Feedback

Providing meaningful, productive feedback for each of the four generations can also be challenging for a manager. The Veterans generation tends to think that no news is good news and may consider feedback to be unnecessary, or even insulting. Baby Boomers would rather give feedback than get it, but when they do receive feedback, they prefer it to be planned and well documented.

Members of Generation X often will ask for feedback and need positive feedback to let them know they're doing okay. When a Gen Xer asks for feedback, he or she expects it to be immediate.

Members of Generation Y also require frequent feedback and prefer to receive it in the form of praise. A lack of feedback can be alarming for members of this age group, who sometimes mistake silence for disapproval.

Rewards

It's interesting that studies indicate that, with the exception of the Baby Boomers, money is not regarded as the best reward. For the Greatest Generation, the most valued reward is personal satisfaction in a job well done. Its members, however, also like to know that their contributions have made a difference, so recognition of a job well done may increase their satisfaction.

Baby Boomers, as mentioned, prefer rewards in the form of money and also value title recognition. For members of Generation X, freedom to work as they wish is the reward of choice, and, members of Generation Y value meaningful work as a reward.

Messages to Motivate

These are at the crux of boosting performance, and you'll find it useful to keep these expectations in mind when dealing with employees of various ages.

Older employees, the Veterans, want to know that their experience is valued and that they are respected within the organization. They place great value on honor and being considered honorable, so it's important to exhibit respect and regard for what they've done.

PERFORMANCE BOOST

Although all employees should be held to the same standard, you can't treat everyone the same in order to achieve the same results. So while you may give your Gen X employees, who are motivated by being able to do things their own way, some latitude in the approach they take when working toward a goal, they must be held to the same expectations as all other employees.

Baby Boomers also want to know that they're valued team members and, taking it a step farther, are necessary to the success of the team. Gen Xers want to be told to do their own thing and that the rules don't apply to them, even though, of course, all workers must be held to the same standards. Members of Generation Y are motivated by the promise of interaction with co-workers who are creative, bright, and innovative.

Work/Family/Personal Life Balance

Members of the Veterans generation prefer—and expect—to keep their work and home lives separate. Don't expect spouses to drop off something at the office or to supply a cake to celebrate a husband's or wife's birthday.

Baby Boomers are considered to be work-centric, with their self-worth tied to their job status and performance. They don't mind working long days and weeks, and they are used to sacrificing family or personal time for work. They tend toward an "I'm always available" attitude.

Members of generations X and Y, however, strive for balance in their work and personal lives. They will work to finish a job so they can leave on time, and they tend to keep their work and personal lives separate.

Understanding and respecting those differences in attitudes and values will help you to earn the respect of your employees and keep them happy and motivated. However, you'll need to be sure that, unless there are clear policies in place that establish flexibility in work hours, everyone is held to the same standards, regardless of their preferences. Some companies are successful with allowing employees flex time, but expectations regarding when and how people work need to be clearly addressed and understood by all to avoid resentment.

How to Boost Performance Among Each Generation

In the current work environment, with fewer employees expected to take a seemingly ever-increasing workload, it's vitally important that you hold all employees to high standards and expectations. No one, from your youngest to your oldest employee, should get a break due to age.

Nor should you allow anyone to use their age as an excuse to do or not do something. Older workers, for example, might try to avoid projects that involve a technology they're not familiar with by citing a lack of computer savvy. Younger workers might frown at being asked to sort papers or attend staff meetings, perceiving those tasks to be unnecessary and wastes of time.

CASE IN POINT

One of my clients, a manager in his early 60s, was having problems in his communications with younger employees. He'd complain that they didn't listen, missed important information, were distracted while he was talking to them, and on and on. Once he understood that his young workers had grown up communicating in a much different manner, he was able to flex his style to work with them. The most valuable item in his toolbox turned out to be receipt of communication (ROC). After offering instruction or guidance, the manager got the employee to talk with him about what he'd just related. In time, employees started listening more attentively because they knew their manger would expect them to respond to what he'd said.

Be considerate about your workers' preferences and needs, recognizing that responses to your comments, requests, and concerns will vary with age. Be aware of the reasons for interactions between employees, too. A young worker might not understand why a Baby Boomer seems annoyed with her as she leaves the office precisely at 5:30 P.M.; the Boomer might be resentful because she'd like to leave on time but feels obligated to stay to finish a task.

Especially be cognizant of the manner in which you communicate to workers of different ages. Joking around with someone of your own age might be perfectly fine, but a younger employee might think you're being condescending or making fun of her.

Make sure you act in a manner that's respectful to each age group, too, keeping in mind their values and mindsets. For instance, asking a member of the Veterans generation to participate in a skit at the company's summer picnic might cause a lot of discomfort, whereas a member of the confident and fun-loving Generation Y might jump at the chance.

Keeping employees of all ages happy and motivated is not an easy task, and it's one in which the golden rule does not apply. A 40-year-old manager who treats all of his employees as he would like to be treated may keep other 40-year-old employees happy, but chances are, his 25- and 55-year-old employees will be wondering where they fit into the organization. Applying the information in this chapter to your workplace will help you to keep all of your employees motivated and eager to boost performance.

The Least You Need to Know

- Managers can expect to have employees who span four different generations all working on the same team.
- Each generation possesses its own general attitudes, behaviors, beliefs, and expectations.
- A one-size-fits-all managerial style doesn't work with employees of different generations.
- Knowing what employees want and expect gives you the tools necessary to keep them motivated.

When Times Are Difficult

In This Chapter

- Your changing role during turbulent times
- Understanding how employees might react
- Maintaining employees' respect
- Staying on track
- Restructuring after layoffs
- Encouraging employees to achieve more

If you've learned more than you'd ever wanted to about difficult economic times and challenging workplace conditions during the past couple years, you're in good company. With the unemployment rate in America doubling from 5 to 10 percent between December 2007 and December 2009 due to layoffs, closings, and other factors, workers who are left have been forced to do more with less, all while worrying about their own futures and the futures of their organizations.

Managers play a particular and peculiar role in all of this. Although you're likely worrying about your own job, you're still responsible for maintaining morale and boosting performance among employees who may be fearful, resentful, and stressed.

In this chapter, we take a look at how it's possible to not only maintain employee performance during hard times, but also improve it. It's not easy, but with effective coaching and the right attitude, you can do it.

How Your Role Changes During Difficult Times

As a manager, you were already in a coaching role before the economy took its downturn and many workplaces were forced to re-examine the way in which they operate, how many workers they employ, how much money they spend, and so forth. You've probably noticed, however, that your role changed during this time of economic downturn. You might feel that, in addition to being a coach, you now bear the titles of counselor, key communicator, interpreter, negotiator, and, in some instances, punching bag.

The recession was officially recognized at the end of 2007, but many companies were already feeling the pinch before that. During the time since then, managers have in many ways borne the brunt of changing workplace conditions by having to relate news of layoffs, eliminated positions, pay cuts, reduced hours, decreases in benefits, and other signs of economic ills.

As a manager, you've likely had to deal with employees who were scared, angry, sad, suspicious, and experiencing a range of other emotions. Business is no place for sissies these days, and your role as manager puts you squarely in the firing range between employees and top management. It's not necessarily a comfortable place to be, but, if handled correctly, you can use it to your advantage and come out strong.

Dealing with Employee Reactions to Hard Times

Everyone tends to be stressed and nervous when economic times are difficult and business situations uncertain. So what's the best way to deal with employees who are reacting to the possibility or reality of cuts in pay, mandatory time off without pay, increased contributions to health care, shorter work hours with less pay, or even job loss?

Employers and managers sometimes underestimate the impact of job disruptions on employees, but they can be severe. As a manager, it's your job to assist your employees, not those who have been laid off. As much as you may sympathize with those workers, your responsibility is to keep those who remain as motivated as possible and performing to the best of their abilities.

> **PERFORMANCE BOOST**
>
> If you experience layoffs within your department, your job is to help remaining employees regroup and deal with the situation. Meet with remaining employees as soon as possible after the layoffs have been completed. Tell them how many positions have been eliminated; assure them that there are no more layoffs planned at the present time, if that's true; and open up the meeting for their questions. Don't get into specifics such as who will handle which aspects of the jobs that are open, unless it's necessary for work to continue smoothly, but do say that you'll be working on that and would welcome any ideas or suggestions they might have.

Knowing what sort of reactions you might encounter from employees during hard times, including after layoffs, can help you prepare for dealing with them. Employees who survive layoffs often experience, to different degrees, reactions that are typical of the stages of grieving. These include denial, shock, pleading, anger, and acceptance. Not all employees will experience all of these emotions, but many will experience some of them. It's important to consider each employee, as each one will experience different reactions. In addition to these emotions, employees often experience the following:

- **Fear and uncertainty.** "Will there be more layoffs? Am I next? What's going to happen? Should I just quit and get it over with?" The period after layoffs is an uncertain and scary time. It's your job to be reassuring and try to keep your workers operational and on task.

- **Sense of unfairness and betrayal.** Employees will make their own judgments about the fairness of the layoffs, especially if someone they are close to was let go. You can help by explaining the process used to identify employees to be laid off.

- **Guilt and sadness.** The feelings of guilt and sadness after layoffs are called "survivor syndrome." Employees may feel guilty for still having a job while former co-workers have been laid off and are struggling. Chances are, they miss the co-workers and are worried about them. These emotions can affect not only productivity, but also employee health, and managers should pay close attention to how team members seem to be handling the situation.

- **Resentment.** Like anger, resentment is an appropriate and understandable reaction to layoffs. Friends and co-workers are gone, everyone is expected to take on more work, and no one is certain of what might happen. The workplace has been severely disrupted, and it could take months before a new normal has set in.

- **Gratitude and possible optimism.** Some employees will be happy to have made the cut and will respond with optimism, even if not immediately. Those workers who are able to look ahead will recover more quickly and will begin to move on, perhaps even enjoying the additional responsibilities and challenges.

These reactions will vary from person to person and will last for varying amounts of time. Being aware of what's going on will help you maintain patience and practice understanding as you work to get team members moving forward.

How to Maintain Employee Respect

The best way to maintain the respect of employees when the ship appears to be sinking is to be honest with them. They're probably not getting much information from the top, which can lead to speculation, rumors, and mistrust. You need to provide honest information based on your understanding of the situation.

Traditionally, top management decides on a course of action and relates it to middle managers. Those in the middle often have to pass along that information. If you find yourself in that position, be up front and share as much information as you're able to, but don't be tempted to share news that's confidential or otherwise off limits. You may find yourself wanting to be helpful to employees by telling them what they can expect and being candid about the organization's situation, but be mindful of constraints handed down from top management.

PERFORMANCE BOOST

Possessing information that affects workers and being unable to share it with them is a difficult situation for managers who genuinely care about their employees and sympathize with their situations. If someone asks you whether he's going to be laid off, practice active listening by saying something like, "I can understand that you're worried about this" and allowing him to express his concerns. Don't, however, confirm a layoff, even if you have that information. Simply tell the employee that you're not able to share any more information than you have, and encourage him to continue working.

If possible, speak to small groups of employees, addressing their concerns and answering questions. Try to put to rest any rumors or misinformation, and be as optimistic as you're able to. However, don't try to sugarcoat the situation by telling workers not to worry or assuring them that everything will be okay. Even if you know (or think you know) that a certain employee or department will not be affected, don't share that information, no matter how much you'd like to be reassuring. Situations can change quickly during economic downturns and it would be disastrous for you to tell an employee you knew for a fact she wouldn't be laid off, only to have the tables turn a week later and the employee let go.

Hopefully everything *will* be okay, but employees who are frightened about losing their jobs don't want to be advised not to worry.

How to Keep Yourself and Employees on Track

The last thing you want in your workplace is to have employees spending their time anticipating what might happen, spreading and discussing rumors, or speculating about what has already happened. You need your employees to stay on track and keep working. If you've experienced layoffs or other cuts, employee performance becomes increasingly important as you struggle to maintain production levels with fewer employees.

But how can you keep employees motivated if they've watched co-workers get laid off and are afraid for their own jobs and suspicious about the intentions of the organization? Your job as a manager may never be as difficult, or as important, as it is when the workplace environment is in this state.

Be Visible and Available

Even if you're busier than ever figuring out how to move your team forward following layoffs, resist the temptation to go into your office and shut the door. Peace and quiet is nice, but now isn't the time for it. Avoiding direct and frequent interaction with employees during this time is a big mistake that will result in negative consequences down the road.

You might think that they'd prefer for you to disappear, but your employees need you to be visible and available to them. Your presence will help hold your team together when times are tough. Be sure they know that you're available to hear their concerns, but don't wait for them to come to you. Make it a point to ask employees how they're doing, especially any whom you've heard are struggling.

Walk around and touch base, or consider arranging for small group sit-downs over lunch, during which time workers can ask questions or talk about their concerns. You need to know what they need, and they need to know that you're there for them and can be counted on.

Stay Positive, but Don't Be Fake

As difficult as it might be, you've got to remain upbeat and positive during tough times, to help maintain morale and keep employees performing at acceptable levels. And you've got to pass that positive attitude along to your workers. Keep the following tips in mind as you work to maintain your own positive attitude and keep your team's morale at acceptable levels:

- Let employees know that they're appreciated. A sincere "thank you" goes a long way under normal circumstances and is even more important when times are uncertain and employees are stressed.

- Don't predict more hard times, even if you know they're coming. If you have knowledge of further cuts or layoffs, or even the possibility of such, keep this to yourself as you and your employees navigate day-to-day operations.

- Don't assure employees that all is well or that everything will be fine. Your team understands that times aren't good and will write you off as insincere if you try to sugarcoat the situation. Acknowledge the difficulties, but don't let anyone buy into despair. Maintain a hopeful attitude and look ahead to better times.

Keep Your Business Running

As important as it is for you to be available, concerned, and interested during difficult times, it's also your job to ensure that business continues as usual. Allowing tasks to go unfinished or job performance to slide will only add to a difficult situation as the consequences of the neglect become known.

Encourage employees to remain invested in their jobs and the organization by asking them to share their ideas for maintaining production levels with fewer people or increasing efficiency. Continue to share the news that you can from upper management, and involve your workers in the day-to-day operations of the organization. Encourage them to take ownership of any additional work that might be necessary for them to assume, pointing out the opportunity to learn new skills and increase knowledge.

Team members might initially resent having to take on additional work, but assuring them that you're on their side and willing to help them learn what they need to know will go a long way in making sure that work gets done and that the organization is able to move forward.

Regrouping After Layoffs or Other Changes

If you experience layoffs or other major changes within your department, good communication is essential. Your employees will be uncertain and will be looking for guidance from you.

Convene a meeting of your team as soon as possible after layoffs occur, and tell employees what they should expect to happen in the coming days and weeks. Make arrangements for immediate needs to be met, and explain that you're working to set up a transition plan to keep the department operating smoothly. Tell employees that you'll be seeking their input as you move forward and that you're available to meet with anyone who has concerns or questions. An open door policy is extremely important in maintaining a level of trust with workers who might be feeling anxious, sad, and stressed.

PERFORMANCE BOOST

Even if you weren't involved in the decision making regarding layoffs, you might encounter deep resentment and mistrust from employees who remain. Layoff survivors experience a range of intense emotions and need someone to direct them toward. Since they have more contact with you than the higher-ups who were more directly involved in the layoff decisions, you could bear the brunt of their anger and resentment. If this occurs, keep the channels of communication open and let them talk about how they're feeling. Be dependable and reliable, and eventually you'll regain their trust.

Rethinking Job Descriptions

Before your staff has even gotten used to the idea that layoffs have occurred and some of their co-workers and friends are no longer present, you'll need to be rethinking job descriptions and how the employees who are left can meet the responsibilities of the department.

This isn't an easy task and will require a good deal of thought and planning. If you can, it's a good idea to involve your employees in this job, or at least get them invested in the idea of taking on additional responsibilities. Letting them have some say in how the additional work should be handled gives them some ownership and makes them feel that they're still valuable team members. Remember that although job descriptions tell employees what they are to do, they don't provide instruction on how to do it or why they do it. Reassigning work based on job descriptions is just the first part of your work.

Rethinking Standards and Expectations

You'll need to rethink and re-establish job standards and expectations for employees who are taking over the work of a co-worker who's been laid off. Don't assume that employees who have worked in your department for some time automatically understand the expectations for a job they haven't performed previously. Review Chapter 3 to go over all the considerations that should be included in an explanation of job standards and expectations, and make sure those considerations are fully explained to employees who are assuming new job responsibilities.

Although you're in a hurry to move the department along and get every job covered, remember that even experienced employees will require time to learn and become accustomed to new tasks and responsibilities.

CASE IN POINT

Mike managed a department of eight employees, but then three of them were laid off, leaving five. He tried hard to redistribute the work of those who had been let go, working with remaining employees to revise job descriptions, establish creditable job expectations, and provide additional training when necessary. Weeks went by, and Mike grew increasingly frustrated with his workers, who seemed to be sluggish and unmotivated to perform well. Mike didn't realize that employees can feel the effects of layoffs for weeks, or even months, after they occur. When advised by a human resources person how to handle the situation, Mike developed more patience and was able to work more closely with employees who needed extra attention.

Do Employees Need More Training?

An employee who is taking on new tasks and responsibilities will likely require some degree of training in order to succeed. Even if it's just a matter of having you or another employee walking the worker through the task, you shouldn't assume that someone knows how to perform a new job.

Training may not be encouraged in a workplace looking to trim expenses and keep costs down, but denying it is counterproductive and can result in further demoralization of employees.

Getting employees back on their feet and ready to work following layoffs or other major disruptions is a big challenge for managers, requiring both time and attention. You'll need to be an advocate for employees, to ensure that they have the time and training necessary for learning new skills, brushing up on jobs they may not have done for a long time, and learning how to work together in a different dynamic.

Using a Downsized Environment to Boost Employee Performance

As unlikely as it sounds, a downsized environment can be a great opportunity for getting employees motivated and boosting performance. Whether that happens, however, depends on how you handle the situation.

Following layoffs, it's important to remind workers of the company's vision, goals, and mission. It's equally important to acknowledge that those things might have changed and need to be redefined. Goals may have had to change to accommodate economic realities, and the company's vision of the future may look different than it did six months or a year ago.

Help employees understand that the organization will have to change and reorganize. There could be a new reporting structure or other changes. Work with employees to establish a clear picture of where the organization is and where it's headed, or hopes to be headed. Spend extra time with workers, and be willing to talk frankly with them about what needs to be done to bring the department up to full capacity with fewer team members performing more work.

Plan events or activities to help build morale and promote camaraderie and teamwork. Pay extra attention to rewards and recognition for good work; nonmonetary rewards (see Chapter 18) can cost little and go a long way toward keeping employees motivated. Also be sure that employees understand the opportunities that can be found in a downsized workplace.

Increased Opportunities for Invested Workers

Workers who are willing to explore new possibilities and try out new areas of work are likely to discover a variety of opportunities waiting for them. Motivated workers will understand that fewer employees mean additional job opportunities and will want to fill the spots left open. An employee may have an opportunity to move up the ladder to a higher position left open after downsizing. Another worker might be moved into a managerial spot that was left vacant. Additional responsibility may be given to invested employees, raising their value to the organization and positioning them for advancement. As a manager, it's your job to help team members understand this and to advise them on how to move ahead.

A Quicker Climb up the Ladder

With fewer employees in the organizational chain, there may be some empty rungs on the ladder. Employees who are willing to work hard and seek opportunity often are moved into higher positions that need to be filled, meaning that they may advance their careers far more quickly than they would have otherwise.

CASE IN POINT

Ashley joined a large marketing firm less than a year before layoffs hit. Just a year and a half out of college, she survived the cuts, went through the company's reorganization, and refocused her efforts. To her surprise and delight, she began getting assignments she wouldn't have dreamed about before the layoffs. She was sent from New York to California to meet with clients, was invited to participate in strategy meetings, and was given far more responsibility with accounts. Ashley embraced these opportunities and rose to the occasion, rocketing her career to a level she had never expected to achieve so soon.

Employees who look for opportunities and aren't shy about asking for what's available stand a good chance in a downsized environment of moving up the ladder in a manner that would not have occurred without downsizing. Again, it's your job to guide them and use these opportunities as a means of motivating and boosting performance.

Building a Resumé in a Downsized Environment

Taking on more work after downsizing occurs gives employees opportunities to develop new skills and acquire additional knowledge. This leads to new opportunities that help them build their resumé in an accelerated fashion.

A job or position that may have taken two years to achieve during ordinary times may take only six months in a downsized environment. Your organization is likely looking for employees who bring new ideas, are willing to be involved in decision making, and are eager to help move the company forward, so be sure your motivated workers are aware of this and involved. Loading up their resumés during periods such as this will strongly position employees to move ahead within your organization when the economic situation improves.

The Least You Need to Know

- You need to be ready to change your role as manager during troubled economic times.
- Excellent communication is imperative following layoffs or other major disruptions.
- Employees will look to you for direction in hard times.
- Plan to be available to employees as you work to get business back on track.
- You and your team may discover good opportunities in down-sized environments.

The Status Quo

In This Chapter

- Challenges of good times
- Recognizing complacency
- Consequences of complacency
- Keeping employees motivated

One would hope that, once the economy gets back on track after this long recession, the unemployment rate settles at a reasonable level, layoffs become a past trend, and employers are hiring new workers again, we'd breathe a collective sigh of relief and watch our businesses excel and prosper. You'd think that, under those circumstances, without the looming threat of layoffs or other major disruptions, employees would be motivated to kick off in high gear, meeting and exceeding expectations like never before.

Well, hopefully, that will be the case. However, as in many instances, we tend to have short memories, and hard times in the workplace soon become distant memories as employees readjust to prosperity and job security.

Managing in good times can be nearly as challenging as managing during recession, layoffs, and uncertainty. The challenges are different, but they remain. In this chapter, we take a look at what those challenges are and explore how you can recognize them and keep your employees from settling into complacency.

Keeping Employees Motivated During Good Times

When times are tough, everybody is on edge, waiting to see what's going to happen next. If your organization is spared cuts and downsizings, the one next door or across the street may not be, and nobody knows who might be next. Owners are nervous, managers are nervous, and employees are nervous. This creates its own set of management problems, but complacency isn't one of them.

When times are good, however, everyone tends to be more relaxed and at ease. It might not seem quite as important for an order to get out to a customer on time, or a report to get filed by the deadline, or the walk-in cooler to get cleaned exactly according to specification. Everybody is pretty sure about their jobs, paychecks are scheduled for every Friday, and it's all good.

Except that it's *not* all good. A sense of security at work is a good thing, but when it becomes overblown, you're at risk for employee complacency, which is a bad thing.

PERFORMANCE BOOST

During good times, it's increasingly important to keep employees focused on what's ahead and remind them of upcoming challenges. Don't let them get too firmly entrenched in the day-to-day stuff—that tends to result in a lack of excitement and decreased motivation.

Complacency occurs when employees settle into their surroundings to the point that they don't feel a sense of urgency about anything. At the same time, they're not keeping their eyes on the big picture of organizational goals or scrambling to address problems and issues. They're just coasting along, doing what they need to get by, and they're out the door at 5:30 sharp.

Recognizing Signs of Complacency

Complacency may be most often addressed in terms of safety and the risks associated with complacent workers. However, it also affects other aspects of the workplace, such as morale and employee satisfaction. Complacency is also bad for business in terms of customer satisfaction, productivity, and nearly every other area you can think of.

Complacency can show up in many forms and manifests with a variety of symptoms, ranging from bickering and complaining among employees to increased absenteeism. Let's look at some of the most common signs of employee complacency.

Boredom

If your employees are bored at work, you've got a problem as a manager. With the great multitude of distractions available to employees, a bored workforce will have no problem finding things other than work to do. Just type "bored workers" into a search engine, and you'll find plenty of sites designed just for that segment of the population.

PERFORMANCE GAP

If your organization doesn't have controls in place for web browsing during work hours, you probably should consider doing so. Non-work-related Internet use is one of the biggest distractions cited by employees, resulting in billions of dollars of lost productivity each year. Be aware, however, that some software programs have add-ons that can camouflage pages employees don't want you to see, making their screens appear to be businesslike and work related as you walk by.

And while having your bored employees Twittering, texting, and hanging out on bored worker websites during work hours is bad enough, it actually is preferable to them meeting with clients, handling customer service calls, or dealing with suppliers. Bored employees don't inspire excitement, or even interest, among customers and associates. They're a turnoff, and that's the last thing you want to do to customers.

Increased Number of Mistakes

Complacent workers aren't all that interested in anything, including diligently completing their work or checking the work once it's finished. As a result, you'll see an increased number of mistakes coming from complacent workers, and so will your customers, competitors, and supervisors.

That's not to say that mistakes don't occur when employees aren't complacent. You can bet there were plenty of mistakes during the downsizing days, when it seemed like every worker was trying to do the jobs of three, but mistakes due to complacency are different. They result from disinterest or carelessness rather than time constraints. And they're usually far more avoidable. If you're noticing an increased rate of mistakes among your employees, it's worth checking into the complacency level.

Lack of Creativity

Once complacency sets in, imagination and creativity tend to suffer. Bored employees aren't known for tossing around ideas on how they can increase output, serve customers better, or improve their working environment. They're more likely to be taking personal calls or checking cheap flights online.

Creativity is necessary for your workplace to prosper. It's the impetus for good ideas, better ideas, and great ideas. It lets employees look at problems as puzzles to be figured and solved, not situations they have to live with. Creativity breeds excitement and fun, and it staves off dullness and boredom. When creativity suffers, most other aspects of the workplace do, too.

CASE IN POINT

Linda loved her job in the florist shop, primarily because she was encouraged to come up with different arrangements for the displays and be as creative as possible when putting together floral arrangements. When her manager moved away and a new one was brought in, however, everything changed. Linda was no longer encouraged, or even allowed, to be creative with the window displays, and floral arrangements were only to be done by the book. Knowing that she wasn't encouraged to be creative caused Linda to become dispirited and complacent, which led to even less creativity and significantly impacted her job performance.

There's an attitude that creativity and work aren't compatible, and that employees should simply show up and do what they're assigned to do. Nothing, however, could be further from the truth. Employees should be encouraged to be creative, for creativity results in better methods and higher achievement. If complacency has led to decreased creativity within your organization, it's time to address the issue.

Decreased Productivity

Decreased productivity goes hand in hand with boredom, increased incidence of mistakes, and lack of creativity, and it's yet another symptom of complacency. Productivity can drop for other reasons as well, including stress among employees, increased absenteeism, and dissatisfaction, but complacency can cause productivity to drop pretty much across the board. When productivity decreases, all areas of your organization are affected.

Consequences of Complacency

When times are good and nobody is worried, employees and management alike might be content to look inward or see only what's going on in their immediate sphere. This is dangerous because it limits vision and causes team members to lose sight of where they're trying to go.

Complacency can start out small and benign, but it tends to spread, eventually affecting an entire department or even the whole organization. The consequences of this are detrimental. Let's take a look at some of the things that happen in the workplace when complacency sets in.

Team Members Lose Sight of Company Goals and Mission

You might remember from Chapter 2 that in the center of the performance management cycle are the customer and the mission of the organization. The company mission, along with its goals, has to be at the center of employees' efforts and the source of their motivation to meet or exceed job performance expectations.

When workers become complacent, however, they stop thinking about their mission, and their goals become short-sighted and uninspiring. And when goals are uninspiring, work becomes uninspiring and workers get uninspired. Uninspired workers don't inspire co-workers, customers, or anyone else they meet, and the organization suffers.

If you feel that your employees have lost sight of the organization's goals and mission, begin a campaign to raise awareness. Remember that goals should be clear, understandable, and measurable, and the mission of the company should be easy to understand and somewhat attainable. The goals need to be spelled out and clarified, and workers need to let you know they understand.

Quality of Work Decreases

When the number of mistakes increases and creativity and productivity levels decrease, the overall quality of work within your organization certainly will suffer. This causes problems even in good times, because there still are competitors who would like nothing more than to claim your best customers as their own.

You need to address a decrease in the quality of work among your employees quickly and decisively, as soon as you notice it. Employees need to be challenged to improve work quality quickly. Restate expectations for job performance and make it clear to employees that they are to at least meet, and preferably exceed, expectations.

Customer Dissatisfaction Increases

Decreased work quality resulting from more mistakes, bored employees, and lack of creativity and productivity will quickly lead to increased customer dissatisfaction. How could that not be the result?

A customer who orders nine cases of paper and receives only six cases is not a satisfied customer. Nor is the customer who needed the display done by 5 P.M. Wednesday because he was leaving at 7 P.M. for a trade show, only to find out Wednesday morning that it won't be ready until the next day. The customer who gets short-changed at the cash register, the online shopper whose order doesn't get shipped on time, and the frequent flyer who misses an important meeting due to flight delays aren't happy customers, either.

To compound the problem, complacent workers whose actions and attitudes can result in decreased customer satisfaction often aren't overly concerned about the problem. They can't see how that lack of satisfaction affects the organization and, as a result, threatens to impact their jobs. Employee complacency and lack of customer satisfaction go hand in hand, with each feeding off the other.

> **CASE IN POINT**
>
> A car dealership with several locations in and around a midsized city has a policy that customer service employees must follow up on every service transaction. Long-time customers got used to this service and appreciated the effort. For some reason, customer service representatives became complacent about making these calls, and their manager let it slide. A customer ran into the president of the dealership at a community event and told him she hadn't received a follow-up call after her last two visits. The president wasn't happy to hear this news and the manager was disciplined. The president had to do the job of the manager, who shouldn't have tolerated the complacency in the first place.

Increased Turnover

Employees who are bored, who lack in creativity, and who don't engage in the future of the organization are far more likely to walk out the door when another opportunity arises than workers who are tuned in to the company's goals and encouraged to creatively contribute to those goals.

Most employees really want to feel invested in their jobs and perform up to their levels of ability, but if the workplace culture is one of complacency and disengagement, there's little incentive to do so. Then they look for other jobs.

Replacing employees is time consuming, expensive, and disruptive to business. The answer, of course, is to keep employees motivated during good times so that complacency doesn't become an issue. Let's look at the best ways for you to do that.

Tools to Keep Employees Motivated

You've been reading throughout this book about keeping employees motivated in order to boost performance. Hopefully, you've got some extra tools in your toolbox now that will help you maintain a high-energy and productive workplace. As a review, we take another look at some of the most effective methods of keeping employees motivated and productive: increased training, excellent coaching, and new challenges for employees so they never have the chance to grow bored or complacent.

Increased Training

Training is necessary for employees who are experiencing performance gaps due to lack of ability or knowledge necessary to meet job performance expectations. Training also is necessary to keep accomplished employees moving forward during good times.

An employee who is being asked to stretch to learn new skills cannot grow complacent; it's simply impossible. That's particularly true when the training is a means for meeting a goal that's important to the employee.

If Terri is being trained to learn a complicated new software program that will enable her to assume a supervisory level and train other employees within her department, chances are good that she'll be pretty motivated to learn the program and get the promotion.

PERFORMANCE BOOST

Repeated studies show that successful leaders possess certain characteristics that build trust and goodwill between them and their employees, enabling them to motivate workers and consistently boost performance. Those characteristics include honesty, empathy, effective communication, conviction, flexibility, consistency, and direction.

Any qualified employee who is willing and interested in increasing knowledge and skills through training should be given the opportunity, when possible, and then encouraged to put those new skills to work.

Coaching

Coaching is a big piece of managing employees and an integral part of being a leader. An effective coach observes when employees are becoming complacent and intervenes before the attitude is pervasive. A good coach keeps employees motivated by challenging them to do more and to do better. You read in Chapter 2 that coaching is important in these circumstances:

- An associate meets your expectations.

- An associate exceeds your expectations.

- A gap in performance arises.

- It's time for a performance review meeting.

Another key coaching moment arises when you observe even the suggestion of complacency. It's your job to keep your employees interested and invested in meeting goals and expectations, keeping customers satisfied, and doing their part to keep the organization moving ahead. You can achieve that through coaching them, in good times and bad times.

Create Challenges

Another means of avoiding complacency is to create challenges within your workplace. Challenge employees to come up with new and creative ways to handle tasks. Present them with difficult problems and challenge them to fix them. Challenge them to think outside the box.

Employees who successfully meet frequent challenges become empowered and unafraid to face even greater tests. For example, if an employee figures out a new method of tracking shipments that improves efficiency by 15 percent, he or she will likely be eager to tackle another project.

Identify employees whom you believe will welcome challenge, and let them know that you're willing to provide it for them. However, don't overlook employees who maintain low profiles—they, too, may be looking for new opportunities.

While it's true that good times can provide the opportunity for decreased motivation and even complacency, you can avoid both if you're willing to stay on top of the situation. Maintain close contact with employees and follow the steps of the performance management cycle.

Establishing job performance standards and expectations; training employees; coaching; providing effective performance reviews; and keeping the customer in the center, along with the organizational goals and mission, will keep your employees motivated and working toward boosting their performances.

The Least You Need to Know

- Managing in good times is not without challenges.
- Complacency becomes a risk when employees are too comfortable.
- Complacency decreases productivity, which leads to problems at all levels.
- Training, coaching, and creating challenges are excellent motivators.

Resources

Many books, organizations, and online resources aim to improve managerial performance and provide support and direction. Some of those are included in this appendix.

Books

Alessandra, Tony, and Phillip L. Hunsaker. *The New Art of Managing People, Updated and Revised: Person-to-Person Skills, Guidelines, and Techniques Every Manager Needs to Guide, Direct, and Motivate the Team.* New York: Free Press, 2008.

Bateman, Thomas, and Scott Snell. *Management: Leading & Collaborating in the Competitive World.* Boston: McGraw-Hill/Irwin, 2010.

Beach, Lee Roy. *The Human Element: Understanding and Managing Employee Behavior.* Armonk, NY: M.E. Sharpe, 2007.

Belker, Loren B., and Gary S. Topchik. *The First Time Manager,* 5th ed. New York: AMACOM, 2005.

Collins, Jim. *Good to Great: Why Some Companies Make the Leap and Others Don't.* New York: HarperBusiness, 2001.

Dorio, Marc. *The Complete Idiot's Guide to Career Advancement.* Indianapolis: Alpha Books, 2009.

Drucker, Peter F. *Management, revised edition.* New York: HarperBusiness, 2008.

———. *Management Cases, revised edition.* New York: Harper Paperbacks, 2008.

———. *Managing for Results.* New York: Harper Paperbacks, 2006.

———. *The Practice of Management.* New York: Harper Paperbacks, 2006.

Fina, Michael. *Perspectives on Managing Employees.* Florence, KY: Course Technology PTR, 2009.

Grossman, Gary, and J. Robert Parkinson. *Becoming a Successful Manager: How to Make a Smooth Transition from Managing Yourself to Managing Others.* New York: McGraw-Hill, 2001.

Kotter, John P. *Leading Change.* Boston: Harvard Business Press, 1996.

Kouzes, James M., and Barry C. Posner. *Encouraging the Heart: A Leader's Guide to Rewarding and Recognizing Others.* San Francisco: Jossey-Bass, 2003.

———. *A Leader's Legacy.* San Francisco: Jossey-Bass, 2006.

Marston, Cam. *Motivating the "What's in It for Me" Workforce: Manage Across the Generational Divide and Increase Profits.* New York: Wiley, 2007.

Martin, Carolyn A. *Managing the Generation Mix, 2nd edition.* Amherst, MA: HRD Press, 2006.

Maxwell, John C. *The 21 Irrefutable Laws of Leadership Workbook.* Nashville: Thomas Nelson, 2002.

———. *Leadership 101: What Every Leader Needs to Know.* Nashville: Thomas Nelson, 2002.

McGovern, Julia, and Susan Shelly. *The Happy Employee: 101 Ways for Managers to Attract, Retain, and Inspire the Best and Brightest.* Avon, MA: Adams Media, 2008.

Nelson, Bob. *1001 Ways to Reward Employees*. New York: Workman Publishing Company, 2005.

Parkinson, J. Robert, and Gary Grossman. *Becoming a Successful Manager, 2nd edition*. New York: McGraw-Hill, 2010.

Peters, Thomas J., and Robert H. Waterman, Jr. *In Search of Excellence*. New York: HarperBusiness Essentials, 2004.

Phillips, Donald T. *Lincoln on Leadership: Executive Strategies for Tough Times*. New York: Warner Books, 1993.

Schermerhorn, John R. *Management, 10th edition*. New York: Wiley, 2010.

Tulgan, Bruce. *It's Okay to Be the Boss: The Step-by-Step Guide to Becoming the Manager Your Employees Need*. New York: HarperBusiness, 2007.

Watkins, Michael. *The First 90 Days: Critical Success Strategies for New Leaders at All Levels*. Boston: Harvard Business Press, 2003.

———. *Right from the Start: Taking Charge in a New Leadership Role*. Boston: Harvard Business Press, 1999.

Websites

www.amanet.org   Website of the American Management Association (AMA), a nonprofit corporate training and consulting group based in New York City. Founded in 1913 as the National Association for Corporation Schools, it was renamed the AMA in 1923. The AMA provides a variety of seminars, workshops, and other types of training and educational opportunities to businesses and government agencies.

www.bettermanagement.com   Bettermanagement.com is an online collection of articles, webcasts, and conferences relating to various areas of business and management.

www.hbr.org   This website of the *Harvard Business Review* contains articles, blogs, and other resources related to management and business.

www.managementhelp.org   Website of the Free Management Library, an online collection of resources regarding management.

www.promanager.org   Website of the Professional Managers Association (PMA), which represents professional managers, management officials, and nonbargaining unit employees in the federal government. Founded in 1981, the PMA has more than 200,000 members and a mission to promote leadership and quality within the parameters of the federal government.

www.sba.gov   Website of the U.S. Small Business Administration (SBA), an independent agency of the federal government with the goal of assisting Americans to start, grow, and run small businesses. Founded in 1953, the agency provides advice, online resources, financial assistance, and other resources for those starting or running small businesses.

Index

Q-R